The Big6™ Goes Primary!

Teaching Information and Communications Technology Skills in the K-3 Curriculum

Barbara A. Jansen

Illustrations by Christopher B. McCoy

Linworth Books

Professional Development Resources for
K-12 Library Media and Technology Specialists

To Allan, Debbie, and George

Library of Congress Cataloging-in-Publication Data

Jansen, Barbara A.
  The big6 goes primary! : teaching information and communications technology skills in the k-3 curriculum / Barbara A. Jansen.
      p. cm.
  Includes bibliographical references and index.
  ISBN-13: 978-1-58683-292-6 (pbk.)
  ISBN-10: 1-58683-292-1 (pbk.)
  1. Information retrieval--Study and teaching (Elementary)--United States. 2. Electronic information resource literacy--Study and teaching (Elementary)--United States. 3. Information technology--Study and teaching (Elementary)--United States. 4. Information retrieval--Study and teaching (Elementary)--United States. 5. Information literacy--Standards--United States. I. Title. II. Title: Big 6 goes primary! III. Title: Big six goes primary!
  ZA3075.J35 2009
  372.3'58044--dc22

                                        2008045621

Cynthia Anderson: Editor
Judi Repman: Consulting Editor

Published by Linworth Publishing, Inc.
3650 Olentangy River Road
Suite 250
Columbus, Ohio 43214

Mixed Sources

Product group from well-managed forests and other controlled sources
www.fsc.org Cert no. SW-COC-002283
© 1996 Forest Stewardship Council

FSC

Table of Contents

Table of Figures

About the Author

Barbara A. Jansen is the Chair of 1-12 Instructional Technology and Upper School Librarian at St. Andrew's Episcopal School in Austin, Texas. She also serves as part-time faculty at the University of Texas at Austin School of Information. Her latest course is "Electronic Resources for Children and Youth." She consults for the Big6 Associates with more than 15 years of experience. Before becoming a librarian, she taught at Berkman Elementary in Round Rock, Texas. She has had articles published in *School Library Media Activities Monthly* and *Multimedia Schools* magazines, the *Big6 Newsletter* formerly published by Linworth Publishing, and *Library Media Connection* published by Linworth. Barbara holds B.S., M.Ed., and M.L.I.S. degrees from the University of Texas at Austin. She is active in the Texas Library Association and the Texas Association of School Librarians and is a member of ALA and AASL.

Barbara is committed to collaborating with teachers to fully integrate 21st century skills into the curriculum. In 1994 she studied the Big6 model of information problem-solving at Syracuse University with Big6™ co-authors Mike Eisenberg and Bob Berkowitz. She is a major contributor to *Teaching Information & Technology Skills: The Big6 in Elementary Schools* available from Linworth Publishing <http://www.linworth.com>. She recently published *The Principal's Guide to a Powerful Library Media Program* with Marla W. McGhee and *The Big6 in Middle School: Teaching Information and Communications Technology Skills* (Linworth Publishing). Barbara is often asked to share her ideas at conferences and professional educational training seminars for state conferences, regional service centers, and local school districts and campuses.

Introduction

In August of 1994, I studied the Big6 for a week with Mike Eisenberg and Bob Berkowitz at Syracuse University. Before studying the process, my attempts to connect elementary students in grades 2 through 5 (I hadn't yet worked on "research" with kindergartners and first graders) with the information they needed seemed to be a hit-or-miss effort, lacking a critical component that I couldn't identify. I taught library skills and nonfiction reading comprehension skills out-of-context, knowing that the students were not quite "getting it." Teachers brought their classes into the library to learn about encyclopedia indices, dictionary guide words, and the card catalog (yes, I go back that far!). Then, several weeks or months later when the classes actually needed to use those skills for curriculum-mandated assignments, I re-taught them. Students hardly remembered the initial lessons.

One day, while reading posts on LM_NET, a school librarian listserv, I ran across an announcement for Big6 training by Mike and Bob. After ordering and reading their two books, I felt that there was much to gain by studying with the authors. Without much convincing, the school district's Director of Library Media Services funded my trip to Syracuse with the intention of becoming the district trainer.

Thankful to be out of the Texas heat in the summer, I spent seven days at Syracuse University learning from the best. Upon returning, my approach to library instruction was never the same. The day after school began, during library orientation, I quickly discussed the obvious library guidelines to get them out of the way. I then spent the remainder of each period introducing the Big6 to the third, fourth, and fifth grade classes. Using a birthday party invitation as the information problem, I took students through the process, noticing their enthusiastic participation. Teachers who usually sat at a nearby table grading papers were listening and participating. This was different. Without informing teachers (I had been back from Syracuse just one school day) I told their classes that when they came into the library to find information for class assignments, they would all be learning about the Big6 with me, because I also was new to it. Now instead of teaching "library skills" out of context, I taught information and communications technology skills within the process of the Big6, integrating it into the content-area curriculum. It all made perfect sense to both the teachers and me, who, learning along with the students, embraced the new strategy for their curriculum.

The Big6 Goes Primary! encompasses all aspects of implementing the information search process effectively into the curriculum in kindergarten through grade three. I included strategies for third grade because these students are on the cusp of preoperational and operational stages of cognitive development, many not reaching the operational stage until well into fourth or fifth grades.

Learning to Read

By third grade students are expected to know how to read, so the educational focus in primary-grade classrooms is on developing effective attitudes and skills in an environment that nurtures reading. Among many strategies for reading instruction, research by The Center for the Improvement of Early Reading Achievement shows that successful schools provide opportunities for children to "apply what they have learned in teacher-guided instruction to everyday reading and writing and that teachers should read books aloud and hold follow-up discussions."

Implementing the Big6 skills in the early primary classrooms provides meaningful opportunities to read and be read to, exposing children to a variety of texts while children in grades 2 and 3 get numerous occasions to make meaning from a wide selection of expository texts.

Academic Standards for Information and Communications Technology Skills

State, district, and school-mandated curricula increasingly require students in kindergarten through third grade to identify a need for, find, and use information for a variety of purposes. Consider the following mandated curriculum from just two states: Texas and Washington.

Texas expects

- kindergartners and first graders to record or dictate questions for investigating.

- second graders to take simple notes from relevant sources such as classroom guests, books, and media sources in addition to compiling notes into outlines, reports, summaries, or other written efforts using available technologies.

- students in kindergarten through third grade to use a problem-solving process to identify a problem, gather information, list and consider options, consider advantages and disadvantages, choose and implement a solution, and evaluate the effectiveness of the solution. (Texas Education Agency)

Washington requires

- kindergartners to define and clarify a problem by identifying central issues and formulating appropriate questions; judge information related to the problem by distinguishing between fact and opinion and identifying the main message; and solve problems and draw conclusions by comparing advantages and disadvantages, suggesting solutions, and deciding appropriate courses of action.

- first graders to define the central question and ask questions to identify sub-topics, search for relevant information including identifying appropriate and varied sources, evaluate information by locating facts and identifying the main idea, organize information, and apply information by creating and presenting a product that demonstrates understanding of information and central questions. (Washington Department of Education)

Each state has its own version of information and communications technology skills for young learners in addition to content and specific skills for subject areas such as English language arts, math, social studies, science, fine arts, physical education, and health. The Big6 will help educators streamline a grade level's vast number of objectives by combining content, concepts, and skills into a framework that helps children use information for a variety of purposes. This book includes examples of lesson plans incorporating state standards and combining skills and content from various subject areas.

The Big6

The Big6 is a process model of how people of all ages solve an information problem. From practice and study, we found that successful information problem-solving encompasses six stages:

Task Definition
Information Seeking Strategies
Location and Access
Use of Information
Synthesis
Evaluation

People go through these Big6 stages—consciously or not—when they seek or apply information to solve a problem or make a decision. It is not necessary to complete these stages in a linear order, and a given stage does not have to take a lot of time. We have found that in almost all successful problem-solving situations, all stages are completed. (Eisenberg and Berkowitz 4)

While the information needs of early learners are typically defined from an outside source such as a parent or teacher, their engagement of Big6 for the results will lead them in later years to an easy application of the process to personal and work-related needs. After repeated years of using the Big6 in school-related tasks, individuals successfully access, evaluate, and use information for any purpose.

What Is Included

Each chapter is designed to address an important component of the Big6 and its use by teachers and library media specialists with early learners, and it begins with a set of guiding questions to focus your reading. If you are already familiar with the Big6 and have experience teaching early learners, you can go directly to the chapter that best meets your needs. If you have not engaged with the Big6 or have limited practice studying the needs of or working with young children, you should read Chapters 1 through 3 before reading Chapters 4 and beyond.

Chapter 1 includes the rationale for using an information problem-solving process within the curriculum and, specifically, why it should begin in the primary grades. It will provide an overview of the Big6 and how the process differs among early learners, intermediate, middle, and high school students.

Chapter 2 strives to explain the developmental levels of children five to eight years old in order for educators to provide appropriate levels of instruction and learning strategies. Discussion on the effective use of technology in the primary classroom will give educators a frame of reference for meaningfully integrating hardware and software into the Big6 process or knowing when to use crayons and construction paper. In this chapter, educators will also find a possible scope and sequence of developmentally appropriate information and communications technology skills for each grade. Chapter 2 also discusses the variety of ways primary school educators can assess the progress of individual students in each of the Big6 steps as well as whether or not the children understand the overarching question drawn from the content.

Chapter 3 brings all interested parties together for the benefit of each student. It discusses the need and provides strategies for collaboration among teachers and library media specialists. Considerations include collaborating with counselors, speech therapists, special education teachers, reading specialists, and other special area teachers in order to differentiate instruction to help all learners. A section on interactive writing will help connect even the youngest learner with the content.

Part 2 (Chapters 4 through 9) explains each step of the Big6 process and its required modifications to meet the needs of primary-age students. Six major sections of Part 2 will guide teachers and library media specialists in determining the best course of action in designing instruction that is developmentally appropriate for each step of the Big6.

Chapter 4 provides developmentally appropriate strategies for engaging young children in *Task Definition*. The chapter includes specific activities for kindergarten through third grade as children mature in their cognitive development. The main focus is on creating developmentally appropriate problems that address curriculum standards and engage young learners.

Chapter 5 offers activities for engaging young children in *Information Seeking Strategies*. The focus of this chapter guides educators through helping young students identify appropriate sources, including an awareness of Web evaluation.

Chapter 6 presents strategies for engaging young children in *Location and Access*. The chapter focuses mainly on subject directories, simple search techniques, and accessing materials in children's subscription databases and on the free Web.

Chapter 7 provides approaches for engaging young children in *Use of Information*. As most children in early grades will not be able to read and comprehend sources, this chapter focuses on appropriate, effective strategies for educators to guide them in making meaning from information.

Chapter 8 gives ways for children to effectively communicate results—*Synthesis*. It centers on encouraging original thought and teaching developmentally appropriate transferable skills as students show the results of their information search.

Chapter 9 introduces young children to *Evaluation*. It focuses on instructing young children to judge their own results for both effectiveness and efficiency.

Part 3 (Chapters 10 through 12) presents the Big6 in the context of content-area curricula, literature appreciation, and specific components of the school library. It takes a look at the benefits of whole and small group instruction and the use of Big6 Buddies.

Chapter 10 includes an explanation of how the Big6 correlates with state academic standards in the primary curriculum. It contains a section on using puppets and the Big6 Song and Poem to further engage young learners. It offers sample integrated lessons for each grade, kindergarten through third, in a variety of subject areas. These lessons will integrate selected strategies detailed in Part 2.

Chapter 11 gives library media specialists and teachers activities to integrate the Big6 into read-aloud sessions, focusing on genre studies. Integrated activities for popular author studies, biographies, fictional animal stories, and Caldecott and Coretta Scott King award winners are included. Ideas on using the Big6 in story-telling will also engage young learners while increasing their oral language skills.

Chapter 12 integrates the Big6 into the library media program, as most elementary librarians have at least some scheduled time with primary classes. This chapter helps them maximize that time by using the Big6 to teach young students how to navigate and use their school library. Specific lessons include caring for books, understanding shelf arrangement, and navigating the fiction and nonfiction sections of the library.

The Appendices contain tools for use in the classroom and school library for teachers and library media specialists to further integrate the Big6 into the primary grades' curriculum. Primary-level posters, transparency masters, and bookmarks are included. Grades 2 and 3 will enjoy a research journal tailored to the needs of young learners. Two helpful documents keep children in grade 3 organized as they use the Big6 to locate information to weave into their writing and work through independent assignments. An instructional unit planning guide will help you design meaningful units of instruction, and an accompanying document helps you evaluate those units.

In addition, an accompanying CD-ROM includes the worksheets, charts, posters, and other documents found throughout the book that teachers and library media specialists can (and should!) modify to meet the specific needs of the curriculum and individual students and classes.

Works Cited

Eisenberg, Michael B. and Robert E. Berkowitz. *Teaching Information and Technology Skills: The Big6 in Elementary Schools.* Worthington, OH: Linworth Publishing, Inc., 1999.

"Essential Academic Learning Requirements and Grade Level Expectations." 2004. *Washington State Standards.* Office of Superintendent of Public Instruction. 5 March 2007 <http://k12.wa.us/CurriculumInstruct/EALR_GLE.aspx>.

Improving the Reading Achievement of America's Children: 10 Research-Based Principles. 1998. Center for the Improvement of Early Reading Achievement. University of Michigan School of Education. 1 March 2007 <http://ciera.org>.

"Texas Essential Knowledge and Skills by Chapter." 1998. *State Essential Knowledge and Skills (TEKS).* State Education Agency. 10 March 2007 <http://ritter.tea.state.tx.us/teks>.

PART 1
The Big6™ and Early Learners

CHAPTER 1
Overview of the Big6

Guiding Questions

- What is the Big6?
- How do young learners understand process?
- How does the Big6 version for primary learners differ from the original language of the Big6?
- How is each step of the Big6 explained for the early learner?
- When should teachers and library media specialists use the Big6?
- How can teachers and library media specialists decide between using the Big6 and Super3?

Twenty-three first graders listened raptly as the library media specialist manipulated a large lifelike toad hand puppet. In a soft southern drawl, the puppet read to the children from a book about amphibians. Whenever the toad read a passage describing a characteristic of an amphibian, children's hands eagerly waved, hoping to be called on to give another answer to the question, "What makes an animal an amphibian?" The classroom teacher recorded the appropriate answers on a chart tablet, sharing the pen with individual students to help her complete the notes. The reading and interactive note taking continued. Finished with the chapter, the toad asked the children to remind her which step of the Big6 process they just completed. Almost every hand shot up as children shouted, "Number 4!"

The Big6 Process and Skills

The children in the scenario with the hand puppet engaged in a variety of processes throughout their school day. Eisenberg and Berkowitz describe the Big6 as "both a set of essential life skills and as a process" and that it "provides a unified, process-context for learning and teaching information and technology skills" (9). This book's introduction established a need for introducing the Big6 in the primary grades, and this chapter will continue with an explanation of the process and its modification for early learners.

The Levels of the Big6

Level 1: The Conceptual Level

> *Whenever students are faced with an information-based problem to solve—for example, homework, an assignment, test, quiz, or decision—they can use the Big6 approach.*

The broadest level of the Big6 approach is the conceptual or overview level. Here, we are trying to establish the concept of process and flow. Whether we realize it or not, we undertake a process with every assignment or information task. Recognizing the process and our personal preferences for problem-solving can help us be more effective and efficient. As part of this, at this broad level, we recommend helping students learn the following:

- To recognize that most problems have a strong information component; the problems are information-rich
- To recognize and identify the information aspects of that problem
- To realize that information-rich problems can be solved systematically and logically
- To understand that the Big6 Skills will help them solve the problem effectively and efficiently.

Level 2: The Big6

The second level in the Big6 approach includes the set of six distinct skills (see Figure 1.1) that comprise the general problem-solving method: The Big6 Skills.

When students are in a situation that requires information problem-solving, they should use these skills, consciously or not. Completing each of these six stages successfully is necessary for solving information problems. The stages do not necessarily need to be completed in order nor are people always aware that they are engaging in a particular stage. However, at some point in time, children need to define the task; select, locate, and use appropriate information sources; pull the information together; and decide that the task is, in fact, complete.

Level 3: The Big6 Component Skills— The Little 12

Each of the six major Big6 Skills can be subdivided into two sub-skills (see Figure 1.2), or the Little 12. These component skills provide a more specific categorization of the general approach to problem-solving and allow for the design and development of instruction. At the primary level, teachers will not articulate the separation of the sub-skills for each of the six steps. These two sub-skills will usually occur naturally in the course of the process, even though young students will not recognize the distinction. Teachers will include the Little 12 without labeling their existence, as they labeled the six main steps.

Though there is no requirement that any of the Big6 components be addressed in any particular order, it is often useful to define the task before attempting to do anything else. After all, unless we know what we are expected to do, understand the nature and parameters of the problem, and can identify the information sources that will help us solve it, there is little chance for success (Eisenberg and Berkowitz 9-10).

Figure 1.1 The Big6 Skills

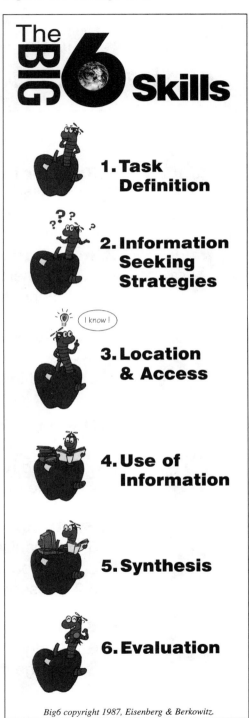

The BIG6 Skills

1. Task Definition

2. Information Seeking Strategies

3. Location & Access

I know!

4. Use of Information

5. Synthesis

6. Evaluation

Big6 copyright 1987, Eisenberg & Berkowitz.

Figure 1.2 Components of the Big6 Skills

Components of the Big6 Skills

1. Task Definition
    1.1 Define the task
    1.2 Identify the information needed

2. Information Seeking Strategies
    2.1 Brainstorm possible sources
    2.2 Select the best sources

3. Location & Access
    3.1 Locate sources
    3.2 Find information within sources

4. Use of Information
    4.1 Engage in the source
          (read, view, listen, touch)
    4.2 Take out needed information

5. Synthesis
    5.1 Organize information from
          all sources
    5.2 Present the result

6. Evaluation
    6.1 Judge the result
    6.2 Judge the process

Big6 copyright 1987, Eisenberg & Berkowitz. Poster design by Barbara A. Jansen, 2000.

Understanding Process

Beginning in day care, students become accustomed to following a set of directions. In kindergarten, teachers can begin articulating the definition of process by discussing the steps used in various activities and explaining to students that they are using a process. What exactly does "process" mean? How can we define it? A simple definition is *a set of sequential steps that when repeated, brings us to expected results*. Merriam-Webster's Online Unabridged Dictionary has many definitions of process. The following may fit our needs: 1) "a progressive forward movement from one point to another on the way to completion : the action of passing through continuing development from a beginning to a contemplated end : the action of continuously going along through each of a succession of acts, events, or developmental stages : the action of being progressively advanced or progressively done," 2) "a particular method or system of doing something, producing something, or accomplishing a specific result," or 3) "a natural progressively continuing operation or development marked by a series of gradual changes that succeed one another in a relatively fixed way and lead toward a particular result."

How do educators aid in developing the understanding of "process" in early learners? Can young children comprehend the published definitions? Certainly not. We have to expose them to numerous developmental examples and allow them to experience and finally articulate the steps of a process. Any time steps are used in a guided activity, the teacher and students should record the steps on a chart tablet or other large display. As the class reads aloud with the teacher the final list of steps for the activity, the teacher asks, "If we repeat these steps, will we get the same results?" The class should answer, "Yes." The teacher then says, "We call steps that can be repeated a *process*. Repeat after me, *process*. Now let's review the *process* of making peanut butter." Many repetitions of recording steps and discussing the meaning of process will help young learners develop their own understanding of the term.

Examples of guided activities in which students typically engage in school that can be extended to learning about *process*:

- Making peanut butter or following any other recipe
- Giving directions for constructing a product (e.g. construction paper animals, booklets, diorama, art projects)
- Preparing a garden for planting
- Cleaning up the classroom at the end of the day
- Lining up and going through the lunch line
- Preparing to exit the classroom at the end of the day and go to designated pick-up areas
- Making a terrarium for the class toad
- Cleaning the hamster cage
- Cleaning up after an art project.

Once students know the steps for various daily or weekly routines, the teacher can periodically test the class or individual students and reinforce the definition and application of the term: "Elizabeth, can you tell us the process for lining up and getting on the bus? Roger, what is the process for cleaning Bumper's cage?" To a student who sits down or plays with blocks instead of helping with art clean up, the teacher may question, "Willa, can you tell me what process each of you must follow when we finish with the paints?" When students understand the meaning of *process*, they are ready to use the Big6 primary version.

The Big6 Primary Version

In upper elementary, middle, and high school, educators will want to study the levels of the Big6 in order to plan and articulate them for students' understanding and use. While the concept of the three levels, as presented by Eisenberg and Berkowitz, remain the same for primary school application, students in kindergarten through second (and possibly third) grade need not be introduced to the three levels, per se. It is appropriate to combine Levels 1 and 2 and omit the articulation of Level 3 in print for young learners. The teacher or library media specialist will address Level 3 in his direct instruction, but he will not include it on the print version. (Part 2 presents strategies for the oral inclusion of the sub-skills for each of the Big6 Skills.) Therefore, a teacher or library media specialist can tell his class "We have a need for information, so let's use the Big6," and then go directly into the six-step process (Figure 1.3).

The goal for young learners is to gain an awareness that we use a process when we need information, and a broad understanding of the main steps of the process.

Other Uses of the Primary Version of the Big6

Third grade students may be ready to read and understand the sub-skills of Level 3 with direction from the teacher and library media specialist. I used the Big6 as published by Eisenberg and Berkowitz, including the "Little 12," successfully with third grade students. However, some third graders will continue to use the primary version of the Big6. In addition, students in any grade who are learning English or who have a language challenge will benefit from using the primary version of Big6 (see Appendices B and D for the Spanish translations). Students in any grade who have learning challenges and who may not be reading at their grade level can use the early learner version of the Big6 with success. The classroom teacher can have both versions displayed, using them simultaneously and in a parallel manner, without

Figure 1.3 The Big6 for Primary-Age Learners

The Big6 Skills

1. What do we need to do?

2. What can we use to find what we need?

3. Where can we find what we need?

4. What information can we use?

5. How can we show what we learned?

6. How will we know if we did well?

Big6 copyright 1987, Eisenberg & Berkowitz. Poster text and design by Barbara A. Jansen.

bringing attention to the students she is targeting with the primary version. She can also change the word "we" to "I" to increase the sophistication of the process for older students. The documents on the accompanying CD-ROM allow for modification of the text.

Comparing the Versions of the Big6 Skills

Figure 1.4 shows the two versions of the Big6 Skills. Compared this way, it is easy to see the parallel meaning in the steps presented to students in grades 3 through 12 and in kindergarten through second grade. The meaning stays the same for each step, while the appropriateness of the language follows the developmental level of the students.

Translating to the Regular Version of the Big6

Third grade teachers should consider displaying and using the transitional chart (Figure 1.5) that includes the primary and regular versions of the Big6 steps. Because most of the students will reach their eighth birthday in third grade and begin entering into the operational level of cognitive development, they should be ready to make the transition to the original language of the Big6. However, third graders do not necessarily need to begin articulating the sub-skills that accompany each step of the process. Notice the chart in Figure 1.5 does not include the sub-skills (Little 12).

When taking students through the six steps, articulate both versions. For example, (pointing to the chart) "Big6 #1 *What do we need to do*, or *Task Definition*, helps us learn about the habitats of animals in our area and how we can best protect them."

The Big6 Skills Explained for Early Learners

Teachers and library media specialists of primary students will structure each interaction with the Big6, methodically guiding students through each of the steps and usually allowing them to finish one step before going on to the next. Teachers and library media specialists design and execute the entire instructional sequence to meet the needs of their specific learners. Each step consists of teacher-directed activities planned around the developmental needs of each student. Of course, much whole-class instruction occurs, but individual assistance, modification, and teaching often takes place (see Chapter 3 for ways to differentiate instruction). The following explanations give an overview of each Big6 step as defined for early learners. Chapters 4 through 9 give detailed strategies for implementing the Big6 process in the primary classroom.

Figure 1.4 The Big6 Skills Comparison

The Big6 Skills Comparison

For grades 3-12 (for grade 3 consider introducing the main six steps without sub-skills)	For grades K-2 (beginning of grade 3)
1. Task Definition 1.1 Define the task 1.2 Identify the information needed	**1. What do we need to do?**
2. Information Seeking Strategies 2.1 Brainstorm possible sources 2.2 Select the best sources	**2. What can we use to find what we need?**
3. Location & Access 3.1 Locate sources 3.2 Find information within sources	**3. Where can we find what we need?**
4. Use of Information 4.1 Engage in the source (read, view, listen, touch) 4.2 Take out needed information	**4. What information can we use?**
5. Synthesis 5.1 Organize information from all sources 5.2 Present the result	**5. How can we show what we learned?**
6. Evaluation 6.1 Judge the result 6.2 Judge the process	**6. How will we know if we did well?**

Figure 1.5 The Big6 Transition between Primary and Regular Versions of the Big6

The Big6™

1. Task Definition:
What do we need to do?

2. Information Seeking Strategies:
What can we use to find
what we need?

3. Location & Access:
Where can we find what we need?

4. Use of Information:
What information can we use?

5. Synthesis:
How can we show what we learned?

6. Evaluation:
How will we know if we did well?

Big6 copyright 1987, Eisenberg & Berkowitz. Poster text and design by Barbara A. Jansen.

1. Task Definition— What Do We Need to Do?

"Task Definition refers to what students are trying to accomplish. The key to successful information problem-solving is to focus on the purpose and need for information" (Eisenberg and Berkowitz 12).

> ## Task Definition—What do we need to do?
> 1.1 Define the problem.
> 1.2 Identify the information needed.

Define the Problem and Identify the Information Needed

State, district, or school curriculum standards dictate to teachers just what students need to learn in any one year. However, the manner in which they learn it is left to the expertise and creativity of the teacher and those with whom she collaborates. One hopes that the curriculum is written by the experts on a developmentally appropriate level, but that is not always the case unless the expectation is an awareness and not mastery. For example, one state's second grade curriculum standards for social studies requires students to identify characteristics of good citizenship such as a belief in justice, truth, equality, and responsibility for the common good—all abstract concepts beyond the comprehension of most 7 and 8-year-old children. However, most teachers understand how to connect young children to those mandated curriculum standards and how to make the experience one in which all students can succeed.

Much of the time, we strive to have each child understand the "big picture," or the important or overarching question, about the content (literature, social studies, science, health). For example, why did Goldilocks mess up the Bears' house? What about these pictures made this book win an award? How did George Washington help make my life better? Why are amphibians important? How can I be a good friend to my pet? How is my life different and the same as those who lived at the same time as Christopher Columbus? As they learn about the main points of the content, students acquire skills to help them understand the big picture or important questions about the topic. Memorizing or merely locating and recording details or facts is not the goal of the information search and may be considered inappropriate practice in the primary grades. When students can demonstrate a broad understanding of a topic, they are on their way to using information for more detailed and sophisticated needs in middle and high school and beyond.

We can begin in the primary grades to help students search for information to gain that broad understanding. On the primary level, understanding a need for information sounds simple, but considering the cognitive level of the majority of children five to eight years old, most won't readily recognize or grasp the need. After posing the information problem and asking, "What do we need to do?," teachers and library media specialists will have to explain the need for information to the students, especially in kindergarten through the beginning of second grade or even later. After many teacher-guided exposures to the Big6 process, students at the end of second grade and in third grade start to "get it" and begin to articulate the task.

Examples of Task Definition—What do we need to do?

- Students recognize a need for information.
- Students demonstrate ability to recognize the problem.
- Students follow directions for accomplishing the task.
- Students brainstorm information needed to complete the task.
- Students refine their list according to their teacher's directions.
- Students contribute to a class brainstorming session to determine the information needed.

What information is needed in order to solve the problem or make the decision? Think of identifying the task as the main idea and determining the information needed as the supporting details. If identifying the task asks children how they can be a good owner for their pet, then determining the information needed helps them figure out just what it takes to be a good pet owner: "How often should I feed my dog? What kind of bedding does my dog need? How can I keep my dog healthy?" Teachers will guide their students to these questions, offering more direction in kindergarten while allowing third graders to brainstorm a fairly comprehensive list of needed information for a given topic.

Kindergartners and first graders will need their teacher to guide all of the discussion to derive a set of questions after she asks, "What do we need to know to be a good pet owner?" Children in these grades may not understand, especially during the first few attempts, what the teacher is asking. Teachers can use these opportunities to model to their classes how to ask and record good questions. They will accept those suggestions given by students, rewriting for comprehension as needed as they explain why they are changing a few words. Second, and especially third, graders can begin to work in groups to brainstorm information needed. This promotes ownership of the assignment and allows students to exert more independence in the process.

Primary teachers do not assume that their young students know what to do when given an assignment or task. They break it down into manageable parts, often giving only one or two directions at a time, as developmentally appropriate. As students mature cognitively, they can follow multistep directions with increasing success. Using the Big6 in the primary years allows for as much flexibility as teachers need in developing and presenting the task and subsequent steps for students to complete.

2. Information Seeking Strategies— What Can We Use to Find What We Need?

"Information Seeking Strategies refer to determining the alternative information sources available that are appropriate to the information need. It's a mind-expanding stage that encourages students to think broadly and creatively" (Eisenberg and Berkowitz 14).

**Information Seeking Strategies—
What can we use to find what we need?**
2.1 Determine all possible sources.
2.2 Select the best sources.

Determine All Possible Sources and Select the Best Ones

Once students understand the task, choosing appropriate sources to satisfy the task makes logical sense. Young learners use those humans around them to satisfy their immediate need for information by asking relevant questions about their world. Their limited experiences in using textual and illustrated sources to acquire information make this step of the process particularly difficult for them to engage. Teachers and especially library media specialists provide the sources they will use (either with help or independently) to acquire needed information.

**Examples of Information Seeking Strategies—
What can we use to find what we need?**

- Students brainstorm possible sources by participating in class discussion.
- Students recognize the need to use people as a source of information.
- Students recognize the school library media center as containing good sources of information.
- Students demonstrate the ability to name electronic sources (online subscription databases, free Web, etc.).
- Students demonstrate the ability to select the best sources from a brainstormed list of possible sources.
- Students choose a recent magazine over a book with a copyright date of 1980 for recent information about the environment.

Promoting these ideals begins in primary grades as teachers and library media specialists collaborate to bring developmentally appropriate sources to children. By third grade, students should be able to list several possible sources after having many interactions with sources throughout their Big6 experiences. Kindergartners will take considerable prompting and guidance to elicit one or two sources, often identifying "the computer" as a source of information while not understanding exactly what type of or the scope of information delivered by the computer. While important, this step in the early grades may not need a large focus, as the students have a narrow frame of reference for identifying appropriate possible sources.

A third grader can demonstrate some independence in selecting best sources but will still need guidance from teachers and library media specialists. He is entering the operational stage of cognitive development and will most likely have difficulty grasping abstract concepts such as bias and authority as they apply to selecting best sources. Kindergartners will almost certainly need their teachers to supply the list for them as they contribute their ideas to the selection of best sources.

I know !

3. Location and Access—
Where Can We Find What We Need?

"Location and Access refer to finding and retrieving information sources as well as specific information within sources" (Eisenberg and Berkowitz 15).

Location and Access—Where can we find what we need?
3.1 Locate sources.
3.2 Find information within sources.

Locate Sources and Find Information within Sources

This is the stage where students find the sources physically or electronically then access the exact information they need within. Of course, this stage continues to require much help from their teacher and library media specialist at the earliest grades, with students showing more independence as they move through second and third grades.

Examples of Location and Access—
Where can we find what we need?

- Students take the appropriate animal book off a reserve cart in the school library.
- Students locate books on the library shelf.

- Students use a children's subject directory, such as *netTrekker®* <http://nettrekker.com> or *KidsClick* <http://kidsclick.org>, to locate an appropriate site on the free Web.
- Students use alphabetical order to find the correct encyclopedia for their topic.
- Students point to and identify the table of contents in a book.
- Students use the table of contents in a book or online encyclopedia article.
- Students use the index in the back of a textbook or library book.
- Students use the "Edit—Find" feature on an Internet browser to access specific information on a Web page.
- Students access the section of a Web page to begin reading for information.

At the primary level, students need a broad understanding about locations of materials because they have not yet reached the cognitive level of independence in those skills. Seasoned teachers and library media specialists of students in intermediate, middle, and high school know that location skills are difficult for many of their students due to the broad range of physical and digital locations of sources needed. Kindergarten through third grade teachers and library media specialists will typically demonstrate and explain how sources are located as they bring to the instructional area the materials needed. Some second and most third graders will have success locating books on the library shelf or using a children's subject directory to locate an appropriate Web site if their reading skills are on grade level. It is usual for teachers and library media specialists to deliver the sources needed.

Accessing information within a source may be out of the reach of primary-age students since it remains difficult for those much older. Accessing in a source the information needed means that students have a good understanding of

1. the question's meaning as written in the task definition;
2. the essential points of access such as table of contents, index, links in an online article or encyclopedia; and
3. the physical layout of the source, whether it is a book, encyclopedia, or Web page.

A young learner does not have the necessary skills or schema to find the exact location of information needed within a source. Why not? Most students up to eight years old (and some older) are learning how to or just learned how to read. This usually means that they read stories (fiction and some nonfiction) for the majority of their reading passages. The skills required to read and comprehend stories varies from those necessary to read for specific information from expository texts. "Narrative text structure focuses on story, grammar, plots, and conflict resolutions" (Texas Education Agency 4). Reading for information encompasses many skills that early readers have not yet mastered or even begun to learn.

Some common text structures used in expository materials are: problem-solution, description, cause-and-effect relationships, enumeration or categorizing, sequencing, and comparison. In addition, expository materials generally use special organizational features such as text headings and subheadings, chapter and section previews and summaries, tables of content, indices, and glossaries. They also use extensive graphics such as tables, charts, diagrams, figures, and photographs and illustrations, many with captions. (Texas Education Agency 4)

As students are learning to read for specific information, teachers and library media specialists will direct much of *Location and Access*, demonstrating those skills that students will gain as they progress to high school, college, and the workplace, but not requiring young students' mastery.

4. Use of Information— What Information Can We Use?

"Use of Information refers to the application of information to meet defined information tasks" (Eisenberg and Berkowitz 17).

Use of Information—What information can we use?
4.1 Engage (e.g., read, hear, view, touch).
4.2 Extract needed information.

Engage (e.g., Read, Hear, View, Touch) and Take Out Needed Information

What information does the source provide? Ultimately, to gain useful and meaningful information from a source requires students to read, listen, view, or touch in some form. We call these processes "engaging" the information, and it is crucially important. The widespread emphasis on reading and its role in overall achievement attests to the importance of this stage (Eisenberg and Berkowitz 17).

Examples of Use of Information— What information can we use?

- Students listen attentively to a Big6 Buddy (see the introduction to Part 3) or a teacher reading from a source.
- Students watch a weather report for local conditions.
- Students interview a community helper for a second grade project.
- Students point to a caption on a picture asking for more information about the image.
- Students read for simple facts.
- Students raise their hand when the teacher reads an answer to a question.
- Students record answers to questions identified as information needed in Big6 #1.
- Students interview their grandparents about life in the 1960s.
- Students give credit to their sources.

As in *Location and Access*, the reading level of students determines their ability to succeed in using a source to gain information. Some second and most third graders will be able to find and use simple facts from a source, but as explained in Big6 #3, the skills needed to access specific information and now extract it for use are not typically taught when students learn to read, because they have interacted mostly with stories, not informational or reference texts. Comprehending stories requires that one reads the entire text and understands events that happen in the beginning, middle, and end of the story. Reading for information requires students to enter the text at point of need and recognize needed information. Second and third graders will need much practice and still not be entirely successful in reading sources for information. Therefore, as students are learning to read, teachers will use many strategies to bring needed information from sources to students' workspace so that they have the appropriate information for a task.

Taking out needed information means that students comprehend fully the questions written in *Task Definition—What do we need to do?* Not only do students need to be able to read for information by entering text at point of need and recognizing needed information, but they also have to take out the appropriate words and ideas and know how and where to record them. This set of skills is difficult for even middle and some high school-age learners. Teachers need to be cautious about asking their students to "read and take notes" until they can ensure that their students possess necessary skills. It may be beyond the cognitive level of most second and third graders to extract anything but simple facts from sources. Certainly we will not expect this from our kindergartners and first graders. Yes, some of the brightest and best readers may reach this level of sophistication in their use of sources, but the vast majority of very young learners will depend on their teachers to deliver the information needed. In Chapter 7 teachers and library media specialists will find several strategies for helping young children extract information for their needs.

5. Synthesis—How Can We Show What We Learned?

"Synthesis refers to the integration and presentation of information from a variety of sources to meet the information need as defined" (Eisenberg and Berkowitz 18).

> ### Synthesis—How can we show what we learned?
> 5.1 Organize information.
> 5.2 Present the result.

Organize Information and Present Results

The key question in *Synthesis* is "How does the information from all of the sources fit together and how can I most effectively show what I learned?" The youngest students can begin to organize their information findings and then show effective results.

Examples of Synthesis— How can we show what we learned?

- Students make a rough hand-drawn sketch before using the computer paint program.
- Students write a rough draft.
- Students organize pictures for a timeline of their life.
- Students incorporate information found in sources into a sketch.
- Students make a final list of sources used.
- Students use a multimedia program to show their results.
- Students add an "About the Author" section to their product.
- Students write a fictional story incorporating facts found in sources.

Good practice would dictate that even primary students begin to learn how to organize and plan for final results. Young students can make rough plans for a drawing, organize materials for a booklet, or write a draft of a story that incorporates facts found in sources. Teachers will model to students the appropriate way to organize information and materials in preparation of the final product, expecting that all students can make an effort to plan for a successful product or performance.

The results of the information search in the early grades will often, as in all grades, be dictated by the state and district curriculum standards. As long as children are practicing the skills and learning the concepts of the standards, students can communicate the results of information searching in any number of engaging ways. For example, students may write and illustrate a story about a tree frog, add pages to a class or individual booklet about animal habitats, use a computer paint program to create original art about a farm or fire station, or write and sing a song about their community.

The final product is not all about putting together the information found in sources, but what the child understands about the topic. How can they show comprehension of the overarching question identified in Step 1, *What do we need to do?* By adding original thought and thinking on a higher level about the information found, students gain and demonstrate a greater understanding of the topic and process.

6. Evaluation— How Will We Know If We Did Well?

"In the Big6 process, evaluation refers to judgments on two different matters: 1) the degree to which the information problem is solved and 2) the information problem-solving process itself" (Eisenberg and Berkowitz 19).

Evaluation—How will we know if we did well?
6.1 Judge the result (effectiveness).
6.2 Judge the process (efficiency).

Judge the Result and Process

How well did I do and what could I do better? Did I show what I learned? *Evaluation* is the forgotten step to achievement, as even young children should begin to think about their thinking in order to improve upon it.

Examples of Evaluation— How will we know if we did well?

- Students judge whether or not their KidPix slide show meets the criteria outlined by their teacher.
- Students use a checklist to evaluate their diorama.
- Students check to see if their project includes their opinion about the topic before turning it in.

- Students determine if their spider book has eight legs and four pages of facts, including one page with their opinion about spiders.
- Students critique how well they worked with a Big6 Buddy.
- Students rate their listening skills by placing a check next to the appropriate smiling (or frowning) face on a scoring guide.
- Students compare the amount of time they spent chatting with friends during the project to the amount of time they should have spent on note taking.
- Students reflect in writing on what they learned about the Big6 and how it can help them in the future.

Early learners have adequate cognitive ability to determine whether or not their results meet simply-stated standards. Young children can compare their product with a model to see if it contains the specified components and content. Kindergartners through third graders can use simple checklists and scoring guides, while second and third graders can begin to rate the level of their effectiveness by using simple rubrics. Accountability for results can and should begin at an early age to foster self-reliance and evaluation in young adulthood and beyond.

Primary-level children can and should begin to rate their efforts in the information problem-solving process. Young learners can mark smiling or frowning faces to indicate their level of participation in listening for information and in working with a Big6 Buddy. As they mature in their writing abilities, students can begin to articulate what they learned "how to do" while engaging in a teacher-directed information search process. If they begin self-evaluation in kindergarten, by second and third grades students become quite proficient in judging their own efforts and determining those skills and attitudes that are deficient or adequate.

Teachers can also provide clear directions and criteria for assessment. This doesn't mean being over-detailed or laborious. It means making sure that students understand what they are being asked to do and how they will be graded. Scoring guides or rubrics are another way to help students assess themselves or fully understand how they will be assessed. Ultimately, evaluation should encourage students to improve and help them to do so. Classroom teachers and library media specialists can work with students on identifying what was the most difficult aspect of an assignment and what they might do differently next time. Evaluation is the culmination of the entire process, but it is often the part of the process that receives the least attention. Teachers and librarians should carefully consider activities and exercises to emphasize Evaluation. In doing so, they actually help students in every one of the Big6. (Eisenberg and Berkowitz 20)

Using the Big6

The Big6 is one of many processes and strategies that teachers will use with children to engage them in the curriculum. The scientific method and the writing process are two common processes used frequently to aid in scientific discovery and written composition. When students need information to solve a problem, using the Big6 makes sense: it is easy to understand and can increase in sophistication with the students' cognitive ability and types of information and results with which students need to engage. Teachers can plan to use the Big6 when the curriculum requires information; however, there will be times when a formal process is not needed. Answering quick reference questions may mean a call to the library or a quick visit to the online version of World Book encyclopedia.

The Big6 and Super3

Teachers and library media specialists often choose to use the Super3 (plan, do, review), instead of the Big6, with very young children. I began using the Big6 with kindergartners, first, and second graders before the Super3 was created. I decided to continue using the Big6 strategies and simple vocabulary I employed with the younger grades with great success. Teachers and library media specialists may wish to begin using the Super3 with kindergartners and first graders, transitioning to the Big6 toward the end of first grade or beginning of second. If educators wish to employ the Super3 for all primary grades, consider integrating various strategies presented in these chapters in the steps of the Super3. See Figure 1.6 for a comparison of Big6 and Super3. For more information on the Super3 see the *Big6 Kids* Web site at <http://big6.com/kids>. In addition, Linworth Publishing, Inc., offers *The Super3: Information Skills for Young Learners* by Michael Eisenberg and Laura Eisenberg Robinson.

Works Cited

Committee on the Prevention of Reading Difficulties in Young Children. *Starting Out Right: A Guide to Promoting Children's Reading Success.* Ed. M. Susan Burns, Peg Griffin, and Catherine E. Snow. Washington: National Academy Press, 1999.

Eisenberg, Michael B., Robert E. Berkowitz, and Barbara A. Jansen. *Teaching Information and Technology Skills: The Big6 in Elementary Schools.* Worthington, OH: Linworth Publishing, Inc., 1999.

Texas Education Agency. *Research-Based Content Area Reading Instruction.* Texas Reading Initiative. Online Revised Edition, Original Publication Number GEO1 105 02. Austin, TX: 2002.

Figure 1.6 Comparison of the Big6 and the Super3

The Big6™ and the Super 3

1. What do we need to do?

2. What can we use to find what we need?

Plan

3. Where can we find what we need?
4. What information can we use?
5. How can we show what we leaned?

Do

6. How will we know if we did well?

Review

Big6 copyright 1987, Eisenberg & Berkowitz. Poster text and design by Barbara A. Jansen.

CHAPTER 2
Developmentally Appropriate Practices for Information and Communications Technology Skills for Early Learners

Guiding Questions

- Why should educators consider the developmental level of primary students?
- What can students in kindergarten through third grade accomplish?
- How can teachers integrate movement and playacting into Big6 activities?
- What should teachers consider when planning for technology integration?
- At which grades should specific information and communications technology skills be introduced?

Marissa's head rested on the encyclopedia as she sighed heavily, "I can't find it. Lawrence has written a whole page on Saturn and I don't have anything on Mars." Upon closer inspection, the second grade teacher notices that Marissa's encyclopedia is opened to the wrong article and that Lawrence has copied word-for-word from his library book, most not even relevant to the assignment. She wonders why the children cannot find and record the simple facts that seem to jump off the pages. The skills the teacher expects from the students exceed their developmental level, resulting in frustration and poor practices. Considering the capabilities of individuals and ages of children when planning instruction will go a long way in easing the frustrations of students and teachers alike.

Chapter 2 offers an overview of cognitive and language development of children five to eight years old in order for educators to provide appropriate levels of instruction and learning strategies. Conversation about the effective use of technology in the primary classroom will help teachers ease the stress of meaningfully integrating hardware and software into the Big6 process or knowing when to use crayons and construction paper. In this chapter, educators will also find a possible scope and sequence of developmentally appropriate information and communications technology skills for each grade, as well as ideas for assessing the Big6 process and its accompanying skills.

Developmentally Appropriate Practices with the Big6

As with all sound early childhood programs, educators employ a variety of developmentally appropriate methods and strategies to reach every child and to offer all children a wide range of educational experiences. Children need an array of experiences and interaction with an assortment of sound methods and materials to make sense of the world as introduced through curriculum. Educators should use the Big6 as one of several problem-solving processes in their kindergarten through third grade courses of study, allowing them opportunities to solve problems in a variety of ways.

While the interactions and experience with the Big6 can help develop all domains—aesthetic, affective, cognitive, language, physical, and social (Kostelnik 237)—the strategies in this book will mostly address those of cognition and language. Indeed, the results of various Big6 interactions may very well have unintended or deliberate outcomes of self-awareness and self-esteem, artistic development, fine and gross motor skill development, and social skills. Still most will have directly resulted in increased content and skills knowledge and language development. Kostelnik, Soderman, and Whiren identify the cognitive domain as focusing on "perception, physical knowledge, logical-mathematical knowledge, social-conventional knowledge, scientific understanding, and critical thinking skills." The developmental focus of the language domain includes "receptive language, listening skills, expressive language, reading and writing" (237).

Accomplishments of Early Learners

As teachers and library media specialists use the Big6 to engage young learners in discovery, an awareness of the capabilities of children in primary grades will help ensure individual success. The National Research Council presents lists of skills that early learners, beginning with kindergarten, should accomplish for success *in the next grade*. The lists are neither "exhaustive nor incontestable" and will vary among children (84). Consider the following abilities when designing instruction for primary-age students and remember that most children may not accomplish these skills until the end of the current grade.

Kindergarten Accomplishments

- Knows the parts of a book and their functions.
- Begins to track print when listening to a familiar text being read or when rereading own writing.
- "Reads" familiar texts emergently, i.e., not necessarily verbatim from the print alone.
- Recognizes and can name all uppercase and lowercase letters.
- Understands that the sequence of letters in a written word represent the sequence of sounds (phonemes) in a spoken word (alphabetic principle).
- Learns many, though not all, one-to-one letter-sound correspondences.
- Recognizes some words by sight, including a few very common ones (e.g., "the," "I," "my," "you," "is," "are").
- Uses new vocabulary and grammatical constructions in own speech.
- Makes appropriate switches from oral to written language styles.
- Notices when simple sentences fail to make sense.
- Connects information and events in texts to life and life experiences to text.
- Retells, reenacts, or dramatizes stories or parts of stories.
- Listens attentively to books the teacher reads to class.
- Can name some book titles and authors.
- Demonstrates familiarity with a number of types or genres of text (e.g., storybooks, expository texts, poems, newspapers, and everyday print such as signs, notices, labels).
- Correctly answers questions about stories read aloud.
- Makes predictions based on illustrations or portions of stories.
- Demonstrates understanding that spoken words consist of sequences of phonemes.
- Given spoken sets like "dan, dan, den," can identify the first two as the same and the third as different.
- Given spoken sets like "dak, pat, zen," can identify the first two as sharing one same sound.

- Given spoken segments, can merge them into a meaningful target word.
- Given a spoken word, can produce another word that rhymes with it.
- Independently writes many uppercase and lowercase letters.
- Uses phonemic awareness and letter knowledge to spell independently (i.e., invented or creative spelling).
- Writes (unconventionally) to express own meaning.
- Builds a repertoire of some conventionally spelled words.
- Shows awareness of distinction between "kid writing" and conventional orthography.
- Writes own name (first and last) and the first names of some friends or classmates.
- Can write most letters and some words when they are dictated.

(Committee on the Prevention of Reading Difficulties in Young Children 85)

Reprinted with permission from the National Academies Press, Copyright 1999, National Academy of Sciences.

First Grade Accomplishments

- Makes a transition from emergent to "real" reading.
- Reads aloud with accuracy and comprehension any text that is appropriately designed for the first half of grade one.
- Accurately decodes orthographically regular, one-syllable words and nonsense words (e.g., "sit," "zot,") using print-sound mappings to sound out unknown words.
- Uses letter-sound correspondence knowledge to sound out unknown words when reading text.
- Recognizes common, irregularly spelled words by sight (e.g., "have," "said," "where," "two").
- Has a reading vocabulary of 300 to 500 sight words and easily sounded-out words.
- Monitors own reading and self-corrects when an incorrectly identified word does not fit with cues provided by the letters in the word or the context surrounding the word.
- Reads and comprehends both fiction and nonfiction that is appropriately designed for the grade level.
- Shows evidences of expanding language repertoire, including increasing appropriate use of standard, more formal language.

- Creates own written texts for others to read.
- Notices when difficulties are encountered in understanding text.
- Reads and understands simple written instructions.
- Predicts and justifies what will happen next in stories.
- Discusses prior knowledge of topics in expository texts.
- Uses how, why, and what-if questions to discuss nonfiction texts.
- Describes new information gained from texts in own words.
- Distinguishes whether simple sentences are incomplete or fail to make sense; notices when simple texts fail to make sense.
- Can answer simple written comprehension questions based on the material read.
- Can count the number of syllables in a word.
- Can blend or segment the phonemes of most one-syllable words.
- Spells correctly three and four-letter short vowel words.
- Composes fairly readable first drafts using appropriate parts of the writing process (some attention to planning, drafting, rereading for meaning, and some self-correcting).
- Uses invented spelling or phonics-based knowledge to spell independently, when necessary.
- Shows spelling consciousness or sensitivity to conventional spelling.
- Uses punctuation and capitalization.
- Produces a variety or types of compositions (e.g., stories, descriptions, journal entries) showing appropriate relationships between printed texts, illustrations, and other graphics.
- Engages in a variety of literacy activities voluntarily (e.g., choosing books and stories to read, writing a note to a friend).

(Committee on the Prevention of Reading Difficulties in Young Children 107)

Second Grade Accomplishments

- Reads and comprehends both fiction and nonfiction that is appropriately designed for grade level.
- Accurately decodes orthographically regular, multisyllabic words and nonsense words (e.g., capital, Kalamazoo).
- Uses knowledge of print-sound mappings to sound out unknown words.
- Accurately reads many irregularly spelled words and such spelling patterns as diphthongs, special vowel spellings, and common word endings.
- Shows evidence of expanding language repertoire, including increasing use of more formal language registers.
- Reads voluntarily for interest and own purposes.
- Rereads sentences when meaning is not clear.
- Interprets information from diagrams, charts, and graphs.
- Recalls facts and details of texts.
- Reads nonfiction materials for answers to specific questions or for specific purposes.
- Takes part in creative responses to texts such as dramatizations, oral presentations, fantasy play, etc.
- Discusses similarities in characters and events across stories.
- Connects and compares information across nonfiction selections.
- Poses possible answers to how, why, and what-if questions.
- Correctly spells previously studied words and spelling patterns in own writing.
- Represents the complete sound of a word when spelling independently.
- Shows sensitivity to using formal language patterns in place of oral language patterns at appropriate spots in own writing (e.g., de-contextualizing sentences, conventions for quoted speech, literary language forms, proper verb forms).
- Makes reasonable judgments about what to include in written reports.
- Productively discusses ways to clarify and refine own writing and that of others.
- With assistance, adds use of conferencing, revision, and editing processes to clarify and refine own writing to the steps of the expected parts of the writing process.
- Given organizational help, writes informative, well-structured reports.
- Attends to spelling, mechanics, and presentation for final products.
- Produces a variety of types of compositions (e.g., stories, reports, correspondence).

(Committee on the Prevention of Reading Difficulties in Young Children 118)

Third Grade Accomplishments

- Reads aloud with fluency and comprehension any text that is appropriately designed for grade level.
- Uses letter-sound correspondence knowledge and structural analysis to decode words.
- Reads and comprehends both fiction and nonfiction that is appropriately designed for grade level.
- Reads longer fictional selections and chapter books independently.
- Takes part in creative responses to texts such as dramatizations, oral presentations, fantasy play, etc.
- Can point to or clearly identify specific words or wordings that are causing comprehension difficulties.
- Summarizes major points from fiction and nonfiction texts.
- In interpreting fiction, discusses underlying theme or message.
- Asks how, why, and what-if questions in interpreting nonfiction texts.
- In interpreting nonfiction, distinguishes cause and effect, fact and opinion, main idea and supporting details.
- Uses information and reasoning to examine bases of hypotheses and opinions.
- Infers word meaning from taught roots, prefixes, and suffixes.
- Correctly spells previously studied words and spelling patterns in own writing.
- Begins to incorporate literacy words and language patterns in own writing (e.g., elaborates descriptions, uses figurative wording).
- With some guidance, uses all aspects of the writing process in producing own compositions and reports.
- Combines information from multiple sources in writing reports.
- With assistance, suggests and implements editing and revision to clarify and refine own writing.
- Presents and discusses own writing with other students and responds helpfully to other students' compositions.
- Independently reviews work for spelling, mechanics, and presentation.
- Produces a variety of written work (e.g., literature response, reports, "published" books, and semantic maps) in a variety of formats including multimedia forms.

(Committee on the Prevention of Reading Difficulties in Young Children 119)

Reprinted with permission from the National Academies Press, Copyright 1999, National Academy of Sciences.

Movement and Playacting

When considering how children will present their results in Big6 #5, most educators think of written or constructed products, such as a booklet or diorama. Young children learn well and respond to movement and playacting, offering additional opportunities for them to interact socially and to develop gross motor skills. As often as possible, allow children occasions to demonstrate new knowledge by moving and acting.

Kindergartners can, after studying animals, show how various animals move and sound. After studying simple directions, they can also point and turn to show knowledge of left and right or backward and forward. First graders can follow oral commands from one point to another on the school playground to demonstrate knowledge of cardinal directions. When using the Big6 to solve word problems, second graders can show understanding of concepts such as more or less by grouping themselves and acting out addition or subtraction math problems. Third graders can act out the history of their town after writing a simple script. They can make up a game for first graders to play to learn cardinal directions and teach the game to the class.

Usually the final products of the Big6 result in a show of cognitive skills. As often as possible, teachers will also want to encourage physical expression and creativity.

Technology and Young Learners

School districts spend millions of dollars on technology resources. Board members, administrators, parents, and community members want to know that their tax money is being used wisely. State education agencies often include technology in their curriculum standards as early as kindergarten. Knowing how and when to use technology will move high school graduates along in their college and work careers, as the 21st century workplace demands a mastery of technology tools. Technology plays an important role in schools, and educators strive to integrate it meaningfully into their content-area curriculum standards, as well as offer robotics, Web design, and computer programming courses at the middle and high school levels.

However, kindergarten and first grade teachers sometimes feel pressure to use technology when crayons or pencils may work better. Many students do not have the skills necessary to use the technology effectively, or the final product may better lend itself to the conventional method of writing, drawing, or painting. For a kindergarten student who has not mastered his or her letter recognition, using a word processor will frustrate the child and may cause him to fear the computer. Tiny hands may not span the keyboard and unrefined eye-hand coordination will prevent many youngsters from mastering two-handed typing skills. Pictures created with electronic drawing or painting programs that use a computer mouse often do not represent what the student had in mind, causing a sense of failure or frustration. Teachers will want to exercise their professional judgment to differentiate the technology instruction and use for all learners, introducing components and skills as individual students are developmentally ready. But as with any method or material used with young children, considering whether or not the child is developmentally ready for the tool should precede all state or local mandates for use.

Scope and Sequence of Information and Communications Strategy Technology (ICT) Skills

As most state curriculum standards include fairly general standards for ICT skills, your school or district may develop its own detailed scope and sequence. Keeping within the developmental levels of primary-age children, the tool will help new teachers and library media specialists design instruction that meets the needs of most learners, in addition to serving as review for seasoned educators. For those districts and schools that do not have a scope and sequence, Figure 2.1 offers a suggested starting document for further development.

Figure 2.1 Suggested Scope and Sequence of Information and Communications Technology Skills

The Big6™ Skills	Grade Levels			
A=Awareness, P=Practice, M=Mastery				
I. Task Definition (What do we need to do?)				
determining the purpose and need for information	**K**	**1**	**2**	**3**
A. Define problem				
Identify need for information	A	A	A	P
Seek information related to various dimensions of personal well-being, such as personal interests, community, health matters, and recreational pursuits		A	A	A
Restate task in own words	A	A	A	P
Use a variety of techniques for defining task		A	A	P
Determine if task requires independent or cooperative work		A	A	P
Collaborate with others, both in person and through technologies, to identify information problems and develop plans for solutions			A	A/P
B. Identify information requirements of the problem				
Identify information needed for stated task	A	A	A	P
(e.g. formulate questions, list)	A	A	A	P
Relate prior knowledge to required information	A	A	A	P
Identify probable search terms	A	A	A	P
II. Information Seeking Strategies (What can we use to find what we need?)				
examining alternative approaches to acquiring the appropriate information to meet defined needs	**K**	**1**	**2**	**3**
A. Determine range of possible sources				
Identify print and electronic materials as sources of information (e.g. books, periodicals, subscription databases, encyclopedias, free Web sites)	A	A	A	P
Identify primary sources (people, personal observation, data from survey, etc.)	A	A	A	P
B. Determine best possible sources				
Prioritize according to need		A	A	P
Evaluate sources according to appropriateness (accessibility, timeliness, relevancy, authority, difficulty, accuracy, bias)			A	A
III. Location & Access (Where can we find what we need?)				
locating information sources and information within sources	**K**	**1**	**2**	**3**
A. Locate sources				

	K	1	2	3
Use appropriate sections of library according to need (personal or academic)	A	A	P	P/M
Use online catalog to locate materials in library media center		A	A/P	P
Use call numbers to locate materials on the shelves		A	P	P
Locate appropriate print, electronic, and human resources	A	A	A/P	P
Access appropriate article by keyword or subject in on-shelf and online reference materials	A	A	P	
Use Dewey Decimal Classification system	A	A	A/P	P
Identify parts of a book (table of contents, index, glossary)	A	A/P	P	M
B. Access information within sources				
Use guidewords, keywords, subheadings, captions, tables of content, and indices as appropriate			A	A/P
Scan and skim to access needed information			A	A
IV. Use of Information (What information can we use?)				
using a source to gain information	**K**	**1**	**2**	**3**
A. Engage information within source				
Read, listen, view, touch to engage in the source	A	A	A/P	P
Interview, observe, survey	A	A	A	P
Scan and skim as needed			A	A
B. Extract information from source				
Listen critically to gain information	A	A/P	P	P/M
Use pictures/illustrations to gain information	A	A/P	P	P/M
Dictate notes from pictures or from listening			A	A/P	M
Select information appropriate to the problem or question identified in Task Definition	A	A	A/P	P
Record information (e.g., note taking, drawing, photographing, downloading, audio and video recording)	A	A	A/P	P
Distinguish between fact and opinion		A	A/P	P
Recognize point of view				A
Cite sources	A	A	A/P	P
V. Synthesis (How can we show what we learned?)				
integrating information drawn from a range of sources	**K**	**1**	**2**	**3**
A. Organize information from multiple sources				
Organize information for practical application	A	A/P	P	P
Integrate new information into one's own knowledge			A	A
Organize information from a single source of information into appropriate format, editing, and revising as needed	A	A	P	P/M
Organize information from multiple sources of information into appropriate format, editing and revising as needed		A	A/P	P

	K	1	2	3
Apply information in critical thinking and problem-solving	A	A	A	A/P
B. Present results				
Define audience	A	A	A/P	P
Use appropriate format to creatively present results (print, multimedia products, performances, presentations)	A	A	P	P
Create a product (using crayons, scissors, glue, pencil and paper, children's multimedia program such as KidPix, etc.)	A/P	P	P/M	M
Create a product using word processing software, presentation software, desktop publishing			A	A
Credit sources	A	A	A/P	P
VI. Evaluation (How will we know if we did well?)				
making judgments based on a predetermined set of criteria	**K**	**1**	**2**	**3**
A. Judge the product or performance				
Evaluate the product or performance based on predetermined set of criteria	A	A	P	P/M
Collaborate with others, both in person and through technologies, to evaluate information products and solutions				A
B. Judge the process (efficiency)				
Evaluate the efficiency of the problem-solving process using written or oral responses	A	A	A	P
Devise strategies for revising, improving, and updating self-generated knowledge				A
Responsible Use (may be included in Synthesis)	**K**	**1**	**2**	**3**
I. Materials and Facilities				
Demonstrate respect for materials	A/P	A/P	P	M
Follow library procedure and policy	A/P	A/P	P	M
II. Information				
Acknowledge copyright laws as protection for the owner of the copyright			A	A/P
Cite or credit intellectual property of others	A	A	A/P	P
Avoid plagiarism	A	A	A	A/P
Follow guidelines and etiquette in use of online sources	A	A	A	A/P
Respect principles of intellectual freedom	A	A	A	A/P
Respect others' ideas and backgrounds and acknowledge their contributions	A	A	A	A/P

Assessing Information and Communications Technology (ICT) Skills

Assessing process and skills in the early grades seems challenging and inexact. Even in the upper grades, high-stakes exams and other traditional paper/pencil assessments often do not assess ICT skills because it is difficult to write objective test items for these predominantly performance-based skills. Additionally, expecting mastery of ICT skills from a kindergartner or a third grader may be inappropriate because cognitive development of this age of student is in the preoperational or operational stage, thinking and producing on a mostly concrete level. Mastery of all ICT skills may not occur until well into the high school and college years. However, assessing diagnostically and formatively, instead of only after the learning should have taken place, allows the child opportunities to practice and hone skills before any summative assessment occurs.

Primary students need many opportunities to practice skills and interact with the Big6 process and should not be required to master more than the simplest skills. Teachers should concern themselves more with diagnostic and formative assessments at the early grades, giving students many opportunities to practice ICT skills and engage in the Big6 process in meaningful and developmentally appropriate ways, and helping them to form positive attitudes about reading for information and the information search process.

Teachers and library media specialists should keep a rubric or checklist of appropriate ICT skills for each student (see Figure 2.2) and record progress made by observing students as they practice skills at point of engagement. Of course, a kindergartner will not have as many items as a third grader, and very few students will reach the "Always" designation—as mastery should not be expected until well into middle or high school years. The formative assessment will guide the teacher or library media specialist when differentiating instruction for individuals (see Chapter 3) or designing instruction for the whole class. Library media specialists are in a good position to follow students' development from kindergarten through grades three and higher. They can make adjustments in their instruction and help teachers differentiate instruction for each student as students progress through the early grades. This will save first, second, and third grade teachers time by allowing them to diagnose only the new students each year.

Works Cited

Committee on the Prevention of Reading Difficulties in Young Children. *Starting Out Right: A Guide to Promoting Children's Reading Success.* Ed. M. Susan Burns, Peg Griffin, and Catherine E. Snow. Washington: National Academy Press, 1999.

Kostelnik, Marjorie J., Anne K. Soderman, and Alice P. Whiren. *Developmentally Appropriate Curriculum: Best Practices in Early Childhood Education.* Upper Saddle River, N.J.: Prentice Hall, 2004.

Figure 2.2 Example of an Individual ICT Checklist for a Second Grader for Task Definition *(see CD-ROM for complete set of Big6 Skills)*

Student Name:		Grade: 2		
N=Never/rarely, S=Sometimes, O=Often, A=Always				
I. Task Definition (What do we need to do?)				
determining the purpose and need for information				
A. Define problem				
Identify need for information				
Seek information related to various dimensions of personal well-being, such as personal interests, community, health matters, and recreational pursuits				
Restate task in own words				
Use a variety of techniques for defining task				
Determine if task requires independent or cooperative work				
Collaborate with others, both in person and through technologies, to identify information problems and develop plans for solutions				
B. Identify information requirements of the problem				
Identify information needed for stated task (e.g. formulate questions, list)				
Relate prior knowledge to required information				
Identify probable search terms				

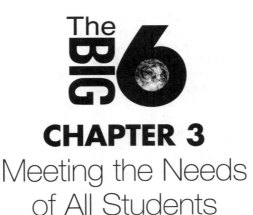

CHAPTER 3
Meeting the Needs
of All Students

Guiding Questions

- How can collaboration among educators benefit students?
- What does differentiated instruction look like within the Big6 process?
- How do specific steps within the Big6 support integrated writing (sharing the pen)?
- How do culturally responsive practices fit into the Big6?

Paramount to the successful integration of the Big6 in the primary grades is meeting the needs of all students and teaching to all learning and developmental levels. Not all students will comprehend the concept of the process, but with patience and careful planning on the part of educators, all students can experience success and gain a positive attitude about information searching. Chapter 3 helps educators consider collaborating among professionals, differentiating instruction, developing culturally responsive Big6 projects, and incorporating integrated writing.

Collaboration Among Educators

McGhee and Jansen define collaboration as

> teachers and library media specialists working together to plan, teach, and
> assess curriculum standards. Efforts can include planning for reading,
> writing, and literature appreciation, as well as social studies, science, health,
> math, foreign language, or any subject-area content. Instruction is usually
> integrated within an information search process framework (such as the
> Big6) so that students will learn the information and technology skills
> needed to acquire the content and present their results. Important in the
> integration of content with process skills is including the component of
> higher-level thinking so that students are required to go beyond the
> information found in books, Web sites, and other sources. In addition, when
> students show the results of the information searching, they should gain
> transferable skills including those of technology, presentation, composition,
> performance, and production.
>
> Collaborative teams will usually include the library media specialist, and one
> or more classroom teachers in any subject area. Ideally, if the school
> employs a technology specialist this teacher will also be included in the
> team. Additional members may include special education teachers to help
> plan individualized instruction for students with learning challenges,
> bilingual teachers who work with English language learners or students who
> speak no English, or any combination. Nurses and counselors may
> collaborate in areas of healthy living and social interaction. In other words:
> Who needs to be involved in this planning so that the most effective teaching
> and learning occurs and every student's needs are best served? (19)

Figure 3.1 offers suggestions for specific duties of the teacher and library
media specialist during each step of a collaborative unit.

Big6™ Steps to Teacher* and Library Media Specialist Collaboration

Big6™ Skill	Suggested Teacher Responsibilities	Suggested Library Media Specialist Responsibilities
1. What do we need to do?	■ Teacher & library media specialist plan together to define an effective task for students ■ Teacher is usually responsible for curriculum content ■ Teacher usually introduces task to the class or may share this responsibility with the library media specialist	■ Teacher & library media specialist plan together to define an effective task for students
2. What can we use to find what we need?	■ Teacher & library media specialist plan together which sources students will likely use ■ Teacher adds sources in which he or she is familiar	■ Teacher & library media specialist plan together which sources students will likely use ■ Library media specialist is responsible for identifying appropriate sources ■ Library media specialist usually solicits input for sources from class and introduces new sources
3. Where can we find what we need?	■ Teacher & library media specialist plan together the most efficient way students will locate sources ■ Teacher will usually teach skills such as using indices, tables of content, skimming & scanning ■ Responsibility of teaching Internet searching may be shared	■ Teacher & library media specialist plan together the most efficient way students will locate sources ■ Library media specialist is usually responsible for teaching students how to access sources ■ Library media specialist will usually teach students location skills related to library resources, including online subscription databases ■ Responsibility of teaching Internet searching may be shared

4. What information can we use?	■ Teacher & library media specialist plan together effective strategies for students to acquire information, such as skimming, scanning, and note taking methods ■ Teacher usually instructs students in note taking strategies, but responsibility may be shared ■ Both teacher and library media specialist may take responsibility to assist students in their note taking	■ Teacher & library media specialist plan together effective strategies for students to acquire information, such as skimming, scanning, and note taking methods ■ Both teacher and library media specialist may take responsibility to assist students in their note taking
5. How can we show what we learned?	■ Teacher & library media specialist plan together transferable and higher-level ways students can show results of information searches ■ Teacher usually teaches skills students need to show their results but may share responsibilities with library media specialist	■ Teacher & library media specialist plan together transferable and higher-level ways students can show results of information searches
6. How will we know if we did well?	■ Teacher & library media specialist plan together how students will evaluate their efforts, both process and product ■ Teacher usually administers to students a self-evaluation instrument, such as a checklist, rubric, scoring guide ■ Teacher shares these with library media specialist so the process can be assessed	■ Teacher & library media specialist plan together how students will evaluate their efforts, both process and product ■ Library media specialist may also share in the responsibility of formally assessing students (the grading process)

*Teacher is defined as classroom teacher; campus instructional technologist; Special Education teacher; Gifted and talented teacher; special area teacher, such as art, music, or physical education; paraprofessionals responsible for instruction; or any combination of the above.

Differentiating Instruction

Accommodating the wide range of cognitive and language levels found in one classroom proves challenging as teachers strive to differentiate instruction for all learners. Tomlinson defines differentiated instruction as "attempts to meet students where they are in the learning process and move them along as quickly and as far as possible in the context of a mixed-ability classroom (Tomlinson, "Differentiated Instruction" 25). "Instruction should be differentiated, not content" (vanSciver 534).

> Each learner works toward a common set of understandings and skills—the "what" or the core, which remains relatively steady. The "how" is the variety of ways that students will reach those understandings and skills, and it may vary considerably. Successful differentiation equals student engagement and understanding. Instruction can be differentiated in several ways, such as by student interest, as each student adds questions that are directed by personal interests. Readiness differentiation occurs when each student adds personal research and writing goals. Learning-profile differentiation is shown in the different products students choose to show their understanding of the key concepts, principles, and skills. (Tomlinson, "Mapping a Route" 16)

Differentiated instruction and the Big6 seem made for each other. While it seems as though all children will be on the same Big6 step at the same time during a unit of instruction, there is no reason students cannot work through steps at an individual pace. In addition, the Big6 process allows for seamless differentiation by interest, readiness, and learning profile.

The Big6 allows for differentiation by interest as students, especially those in second and third grades, will want to explore questions of their own as they determine information needed in Big6 #1. In a study of the importance of animals in an ecosystem, one student or a small group may want to explore the diminishing habitat of a native animal, while another student looks for ways to protect the existing environment for all animals. Carefully guiding kindergartners and first graders to individually written questions also will spark their motivation. However, additional time or helpers will be needed to assist very young learners in the information search.

Readiness differentiation results when each student chooses a step or skill within the Big6 on which he or she has had difficulty in the past and receives review or remedial help from the teacher or library media specialist (see Figure 2.2 in Chapter 2). Choosing materials on the appropriate comprehension level of each student also meets his or her readiness level. Children should have access to books and other materials with various reading levels, video and audiotapes, models, and subject-area experts (Tomlinson, "Mapping a Route" 15). The objective of Big6 #2 *What can we use to find what we need?* calls for selecting a variety of sources. In addition, the teacher addresses readiness through individual and small-group sessions to help students who struggle or otherwise need additional support for the skills required to succeed with each step of the Big6.

Allowing students to choose how to show the results of their information search in Big6 #5 *How can we show what we learned?* differentiates instruction by learning profile. Students express their findings through a KidPix slide show, journal entry, reader's theater, podcast, a book made with PowerPoint or construction paper, or any number of products or presentations. "Guidelines for each type of product ensure quality and focus on essential understandings and skills established for the unit. Students may work alone or with a 'parallel partner' who is working with the same role, although each student must ultimately produce his or her own product" (Tomlinson, "Mapping a Route" 16). See Figure 3.2 for additional strategies that students and teachers may use to differentiate instruction for the various steps of the Big6.

Figure 3.2 The Steps of the Big6 and Differentiated Instruction

The Steps of the Big6 and Differentiated Instruction

Big6™ Skills	Differentiating Instruction
1. What do we need to do?	■ Students identify areas of interest for a topic and write individual questions, which can be added to a common set of questions.
2. What can we use to find what we need?	■ After identifying best sources, teachers will guide students to those materials on their reading levels. ■ The library media specialist can help match individual students to a variety of audiovisual sources, such as video or audio, to address their learning styles.
3. Where can we find what we need?	■ The teacher and library media specialist can work with individuals and small groups to review and remediate location and access skills as needed
4. What information can we use?	■ Students can choose a note taking strategy that meets their needs—e.g. trash and treasure, electronic recording, dictation, drawing, and sharing the pen. ■ Students can choose the note taking organizer that fits their learning profile, such as data chart, cluster diagram (connected bubbles), note taking boxes, note taking folder, or Kidspiration computer software.
5. How can we show what we learned?	■ Students choose from a variety of products to show their results and understandings, such as KidPix slide show, journal entry, reader's theater script, podcast, book made with PowerPoint or Publisher, diorama, story, play, or Microsoft StoryMaker.
6. How will we know if we did well?	■ Students can choose from among several ways to evaluate their success and efforts, such as checklist, narrative, dictation, short answer, or rating scale with symbols (example: happy faces).

Interactive Writing/Sharing the Pen

Developed by educators at The Ohio State University as part of their early literacy program, interactive writing, or sharing the pen, allows kindergartners and first graders opportunities to gain conventional writing and spelling skills as they are meaningfully interacting with content, literature of interest, and personal experience. Children take an active role in the writing process by holding the pen and doing the writing, and the teacher, "through direct instruction and questioning, focuses the children's attention on the conventions of print such as spaces between words, left-to-right and top-to-bottom directionality, punctuation, and capital letters." She asks questions such as:

- How many words are there in our sentence?
- Where do we begin writing?
- After writing one word, what do we have to remember to do? Why?
- Say the word slowly. What sounds do you hear?
- Can you write the letter that stands for that sound?
- Can you find the letter on our alphabet chart that we need to write?
- What comes at the end of the sentence? Why?
- Would that make sense?
- Does that look right?
- Would you point and read what we have written so far?
  (Button, Johnson, and Furgerson 447-9)

Sharing the pen works effectively during many steps of the Big6. When children are helping to brainstorm the information needed for the task in Big6 #1 (see Chapter 4), allowing them to help write the questions on the chart tablet (unlined paper is recommended) gives them ownership in the question development and more motivation to "find" answers to the questions. During Big6 #2, children can help write a list of sources during the brainstorming session (see Chapter 5). Recording notes from whole-group read aloud during Big6 #4 (see Chapter 7) will help children begin to determine appropriate information from a source, as they are meaningfully learning the conventions of writing. Encouraging Big6 Buddies (see the introduction to Part 3) to share the pen during Big6 #4 note taking session gives the Little Buddies a reason to attend the session and a feeling of importance as they "take notes" like older students.

Developing Culturally Responsive Big6 Activities

In our primary classrooms, we see many children of color as well as those whose families speak a language other than English.

> Culturally responsive literacy instruction is instruction that bridges the gap between the school and the world of the student, is consistent with the values of the students' own culture aimed at assuring academic learning, and encourages teachers to adapt their instruction to meet the learning needs of all students. Multicultural literature is that which focuses on people of color, on religious minorities, on regional culture, and on the disabled. Multicultural literature as part of a literature-based reading program, can be used in the classroom to affirm the cultural identity of culturally and linguistically diverse students and to develop all students' understanding and appreciation of other cultures. Integrating diverse cultural literature across the reading and writing curriculum helps students discover the intricacies of language as well as the histories and cultures of various ethnic groups. (Callins 62)

Planning culturally responsive Big6 experiences for all learners includes using multicultural literature and content that reflects the cultures of individual students. When choosing books and other materials for units of instruction, consider those authors and text that represent all children in the class and that expose all students to a variety of cultures. When studying family customs for example, introduce the unit with literature from African American, Asian American, Native American, Latino American, and Anglo-American authors. Have students compare the families and customs in the stories to their own families. Make a comparison chart to celebrate similarities and differences.

In considering cultural differences when designing instruction, educators must take care to plan for children whose backgrounds and frame of references are different from many of their classmates. A student who recently moved from South Texas to Montana, for example, probably will not be able to make a mental picture of a snowstorm during a unit on winter until experiencing one first hand. Teachers should keep in mind the narrow frame of reference of early learners and their varied cultural backgrounds and customs when designing Big6 experiences that meet the needs of all learners while building upon their common cultural literacy.

Works Cited

Button, Kathryn, Margaret J. Johnson, and Paige Furgerson. "Interactive Writing in a Primary Classroom." *The Reading Teacher*. 49. 6 (March 1996): 446-54.

Callins, Tandria. "Culturally Responsive Literacy Instruction." *Teaching Exceptional Children*. (November/December 2006): 62-65.

McGhee, Marla W. and Barbara A. Jansen. *The Principal's Guide to a Powerful Library Media Center*. Columbus, OH: Linworth Publishing, Inc, 2005.

Tomlinson, Carol Ann. "Differentiated Instruction: Can It Work?" *Education Digest*. 65.5 (January 2000): 25-31.

_____. "Mapping a Route Toward Differentiated Instruction." *Educational Leadership*. Association for Supervision and Curriculum Development. (September 1999): 12-16.

vanSciver, James H. "Motherhood, Apple Pie, and Differentiated Instruction." *Phi Delta Kappan*. (March 2005): 534-5.

PART 2
The Big6™ for Early Learners Explained and Implemented

The first section of this book sets out the theoretical framework of the Big6, and, in general terms, describes how it is applied in various contexts. This is certainly valuable, but teachers also want to see how the Big6 works in real classroom situations. That is the purpose of Part 2: to present the Big6 through further explanations and strategies to get started and maintain skills.

Activities for Introducing the Big6 Concept

Part 2 is organized around each step of the Big6. Each chapter (4 through 9) explains each step and provides strategies for planning and delivering instruction to students. The strategies are aimed at kindergarten through third grade, however not all will be appropriate for each grade. Of course, most third graders have a higher level of cognitive ability than kindergartners, first graders, and second graders, so teachers and library media specialists should ensure that all concepts, skills, and activities are developmentally appropriate for their intended audience.

Activities for introducing the concept of each step and skills to engage in it begin each chapter for kindergarten through third grade with or without modification. Additional strategies for increasing students' skill base for each step—a "bag of tricks" from which they (and you) can pull for various information-searching needs are also included. For the sake of the activities, "teacher" refers to whomever is conducting the instruction, whether it is the classroom or subject-area teacher or library media specialist. On occasion, it may be advantageous for a classroom teacher, library media specialist, or other educator to assume certain instructional responsibilities due to their level of expertise; in this case, they are identified by their position.

In introducing each Big6 step to students, teachers should begin by projecting or displaying all the steps in question form, indicating on which step students are working. This allows students to begin placing in context the specific step on which the class is engaged. Teachers may also want to write directly on the Big6 display the specifics for each step for the current assignment. Students can easily understand, from one assignment to the next, that the steps remain the same, while the content changes. The transferability of the process becomes very apparent, even to primary-age children.

CHAPTER 4
Big6 #1
What Do We Need to Do?

Guiding Questions

- What is a good task?
- How does an overarching question help young learners connect with state standards and meet their developmental needs?
- How can you explain "information" to young learners?
- What strategies can connect primary graders to the task?

Designing a good task is the key to a successful information search. A good task

- is meaningful and developmentally appropriate;
- motivates young students to engage in the content;
- allows students to practice transferable skills;
- develops positive attitudes about learning;
- requires students to think and act, resulting in higher-level thought and original ideas; and
- ensures that students add personal value to the educational experience.

Think of designing and delivering a good task as a multistep process for you and your students. Young learners will carefully follow your instruction, but they need a lot of guidance during this and subsequent steps.

Introducing Strategies for Big6 #1 What Do We Need to Do?

Getting Started: Planning

1. Identifying the Content Objectives in Which Students Will Engage

Closely align the content objectives to the state, district, or school curriculum standards. As you guide students through the Big6 process to interact with the content, keep in mind that they should also practice many curriculum-mandated information and communications technology skills, especially as they interact with information and communicate results. Collaboration with the library media specialist and technologist will add additional expertise for the benefit of student learning.

> Example: First grade science
> Compare the life cycles of plants and animals including humans.
> Investigate the life cycle of a frog or toad.

2. Creating an Information Problem and Overarching Question Based on the Content Objectives

An information problem will ensure that students will *want to* and *need to* engage in the content in order to solve the problem. An overarching question (similar to the abstract essential questions that high school and undergraduates encounter) ensures that young students understand what is important about their topic. They may forget or not connect with the details and facts about the topic, but the overarching question will bring forth the heart of the topic, helping students connect to and remember the important concepts. The overarching question can be asked during the introduction of the information problem or asked as part of Big6 #5 *How can we put our information together?*

Even though this step seems complicated and optional, it goes a long way to place the content in a context that has meaning to the student. This also sets the stage for using the Big6 process. The information problem must be cognitively appropriate for the learner. While the problem may be whimsical or purely motivational, you can instead design an authentic problem—one that students may encounter now or in the future—to give the content meaning. Any grade level's content standards can be turned into an information problem.

First grade example: Celestine, the toad puppet, begins talking to the students in the class about how wonderful it is to be a toad and not a human, inciting the class into telling her how much better it is to be a human. She argues with the class about the benefits of being a toad versus a child. Then she begins to get confused and doesn't quite understand why she is so different from the children in the class.

The library media specialist or teacher talks to her about using the Big6 to solve her information problem, "What makes an animal a toad and what makes one a human?"

Additional examples of common topics in primary curriculum can be turned into information problems. The overarching question can be asked during the introduction of the information problem and again in summary during Big6 #5 *How can we put our information together?*

Prehistoric animals: Dinosaurs and other animals that lived before humans are very interesting. *Overarching question:* What is important to know about prehistoric animals?

Spiders: People are killing too many spiders because they think spiders are all scary-looking and poisonous. *Overarching question:* What can we do to help people understand that spiders are good for our environment?

Solar system: You work for NASA. You are the commander of the Pathfinder II that will carry astronauts to Mars (or another planet). You must prepare your crew for the trip. *Overarching question:* What is important to know about planets?

Simple machines: You are the superintendent on a construction site. The newest worker is from another country and doesn't know the names of or understand how the simple tools work. *Overarching question:* Why is it important to understand how simple machines work?

Pets: You want a dog or a cat. How can you convince your parents that you can care for one? *Overarching question:* What do pets need?

Various holidays: We get time off from school and work for various holidays. Why? *Overarching question:* What makes each holiday so important to us?

Comparing objects and events of today and long ago: Show a picture of a wood burning stove and an electric stove. Ask students how the two are the same and how they are different. Tell students that they are going to compare how things were done a long time ago to how we do them today. *Overarching question:* How have the changes in the object or event improved our lives?

Symbols of the United States: Hand out coins. What do you see on the coins? Why are these pictures (symbols) used? *Overarching question:* What do the symbols of the U.S. help us to understand about our country?

Symbols of the state: Show pictures or real objects of your state's symbols. What do these objects have in common? *Overarching question:* What do the symbols of our state help us to understand about it?

School or classroom rules: If we added another first grade class next door, how could we help the teacher and students ensure that their classroom ran smoothly? How could we help the new teacher and students understand our school rules? *Overarching question:* Why do we need rules?

Map skills: You want to invite your new friend over after school. How will you tell his mom to get to your house? Your new friend lives close to the school but does not know how to get to there on her bike. How can you help? What do we need to do? *Overarching question:* Why do you need to know about directions?

Rights and responsibilities of students in the school and citizens in the community: Pretend that you are starting a community on Mars. What are the rights and responsibilities of each person in the new Martian community? Why does each person need rights and responsibilities? What do we need to do? *Overarching question:* What is important about personal rights and responsibilities?

Reduce, recycle, reuse: Show a picture of a pretty pasture or meadow and a picture of a landfill. Ask students: How can we reduce the amount of garbage we throw away? What do we need to do? *Overarching question:* Why is recycling important?

Contributions of ordinary people in the community: Our community needs a museum of people who have contributed to our city over time. Who would go into this museum and why? *Overarching question:* Why is service to the community important to our town?

Natural resources: Show pictures of a lake, pasture or field, wild animals such as deer, rain, rocks such as limestone or granite, or any other natural resource. Ask students if they can figure out what all the pictures have in common. How are they alike? Why are they important? *Overarching question:* How are natural resources important to the environment and to us?

Delivering Instruction

1. Helping Students Determine the Task and Information Needed

Sing the introductory verse of the Big6 Song (see Chapter 10) and have students sing the refrain. Introduce the information problem to the class. Consider using a puppet to help you introduce and work through each of the Big6 steps. Sing the Big6 #1 verse and have students sing the refrain. After introducing the information problem, ask, "What is our task?," or, "What should we do to learn about _____? Let's use the Big6 to help us." Allow students to offer suggestions and list their ideas on a chart tablet or large display. Second and third graders can be put into small groups to brainstorm how to solve the information problem, coming together into whole group discussion to offer their group's ideas (see this chapter for ideas on teaching students to brainstorm). Once students finish making their suggestions, summarize their statements into the task: "We need to learn about toads and frogs to see how they are different from humans and why they are important to our earth." Primary students will need to have the task defined simply and completely by the teacher.

Ask students what they already know about toads and frogs and list their ideas on a chart tablet or other large display. (Use a common KWL chart, filling out the section "What I know." See Figure 4.1.) If children dispute the ideas or suggestions of others, or if a student gives misinformation, mark the item with a star and tell students, "We will look this up to reassure us that it is correct. Sometimes it is easy to get mixed up so we will check that our information is right."

Figure 4.1 KWL Chart

What I Know	What I Want to Know	What I Learned
In Big6 #1 *What do we need to do?* students discuss what they already know about a topic. The teacher records their responses here. Ideas can be categorized into broad topics.	During Big6 #1, record the questions students want to learn about the topic. The teacher may have to reword questions in addition to adding those omitted by the students.	During Big6 #4 *What information can we use?* ask students to summarize or repeat in their own words what they learned about their topic. Best results will occur if you do this after finding out the "answer" to each question that was written in Big6 #1.

2. Determining Information Needed to Do the Task

Once the students understand the task, they must figure out what information is needed in order to accomplish the task. (See this chapter for ideas on how to explain the concept of "information" to young learners, if needed.) Kindergarten and first grade teachers will most likely have students sit on the carpet for whole group instruction and discussion. In partners, young students can possibly think of one to three questions that they would like to know about the topic. The teacher may need to redirect students' ideas to narrow or refine the topic. Second and third graders can brainstorm in small groups, recording their questions for the whole class discussion that will follow. Ask the youngsters, "What do we need to find out about amphibians? What do we want to know?," and have them give their suggestions, which you record on a large display or the KWL chart section "What I want to learn." (Consider sharing the pen with students as the suggestions are recorded. See Chapter 3.) Use this opportunity to teach students how to ask good questions. If students say, "Do toads eat worms?," say, "Let's write 'What do toads eat?' so that we won't have to write a question for each food we wonder about."

When the class has exhausted its ideas, add questions you prepared based on the requirements of the curriculum and the task. Write information needed in question form for the following reasons:

1. The information needed is presented clearly, without much confusion about its meaning.
2. Students become accustomed to finding "answers" to "questions."
3. It is easy to say when engaged in Big6 #2 *Which sources can help us answer our questions?*
4. When preparing kindergartners, first graders, and second graders to listen for information, the teacher can say, "Listen for the answers to 'What do amphibians eat?,'" then read the question again before reading the passage that contains the answer.
5. When helping a second or third grader independently use sources for information in Big6 #4, you can easily say, "The answer to that question is on this page—can you find it?"

Example of questions written for the amphibian study:

- What makes an animal an amphibian?
- How are amphibians different from people?
- Which animals are amphibians?
- What do they look like?
- What do amphibians eat?
- How are amphibians born?
- Where do they live?
- What do they need in their homes?
- Why are amphibians important to us?

It is often appropriate for the teacher to give the class the specific questions that the whole class or groups of students will locate. For example, when studying spiders the teacher may tell her kindergartners that they will find out "What do spiders do that people cannot?" and "What do spiders do to help the environment and people?"

3. Reviewing the Task

For whole class instruction, it is time to review the task and accompanying questions before moving on to Big6 #2. For students in grades 2 and 3, you may wish to put them in groups to study a subtopic, such as individual helpers in the community for the topic of community helpers.

Additional Strategies for Big6 #1
Teaching Young Learners about the Concept of Information

The second part of Big6 #1 asks students to figure out what information is needed to do the task. How do you explain the concept of *information* to students in kindergarten and first grade? We know what information is, but can we define it and explain it to others? Without looking at a dictionary, can you define it? *Merriam-Webster's Collegiate Dictionary* defines information as "knowledge obtained from investigation, study, or instruction" and "intelligence, news, facts, and data" (599). When we first talk about *information* with young learners, we should not expect that they will understand the term. We will need to define it and give examples and non-examples, reinforcing the term whenever possible, before we can expect that students will understand *information* in the Big6 context.

Example: Ask the class, "Does anyone know what the big word *information* means?" Write students' suggestions on a large display. Tell them that it is the result of what we learn. Say, "Sometimes we have to find out information for ourselves. For instance, if we did not know about how to care for our new dog, then we would have to read books or talk to the person at the animal shelter where we adopted our pet. The new ways we learned how to care for our new pet is *information*. People share information with one another through ways such as talking, writing, and viewing."

Each time the class learns new material, reinforce the term by asking, "What information did you learn about _____?" Record the children's answers on a large display, titling the list "Information We Know about _____."

Teaching Primary Students How to Brainstorm

When you ask young students to brainstorm during any phase of the Big6 process, you are asking them to use their imaginations, take intellectual risks, and refrain from judging others—three characteristics that may be difficult for some. Many children come to school not having been encouraged to think creatively and divergently at home, and they will find it difficult to produce ideas on command. Brainstorming can be taught step by step over time.

Start with establishing rules for a brainstorming session, such as:

- Stick with the topic at hand.
- Be creative or practical.
- Include all suggestions.
- Do not criticize or make fun of others' suggestions.

Begin teaching students how to brainstorm with a simple activity such as handing each child in the class a colored block or other item. Tell students that you will ask questions about their items. When others answer, they should not criticize or say anything negative about anyone else's responses, as there are no wrong answers when brainstorming, only some that may be off topic. Ask students the following questions, allowing ample time for students to think before responding:

- What are all the words that you could use to tell someone about how your item looks?
- What are all the ways you could use your item?
- How could you persuade others to use your item?
- How could you convince someone to trade items with you?

Another quick activity calls for the teacher to show a picture of a person thinking—possibly with a large question mark over his head. Ask students to brainstorm about what the person could be thinking, such as, "If I had a magic carpet, where would I fly?," or, "What will I name my new dog?" Students should understand that there are no wrong answers, just creative or practical ones.

Tell students that when they are brainstorming for a purpose, they need to stay with the topic and refrain from inappropriate responses that do not add thoughtfully to the list of ideas. They can be creative or practical in their suggestions and know that others will not criticize or make fun of their ideas.

Teachers can use software such as Microsoft Word or Kidspiration to list and display students' suggestions for the brainstorming sessions in Big6 #1. Second and third graders, as appropriate, can use the same applications to brainstorm in small groups.

Figure 4.2 Brainstorming using Kidspiration for Big6 #1

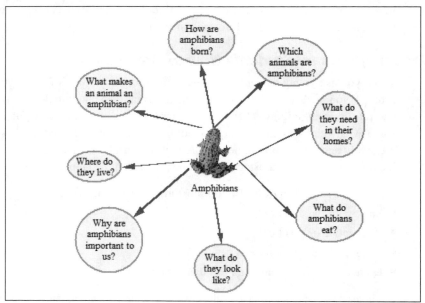

Diagram created in Kidspiration® by Inspiration Software®, Inc.

Showing the Importance of the Task

All students need to understand that comprehension of the task is critical for success. Early primary students can repeat the task to the teacher. Students in second and third grades can begin articulating the importance of the task using this quick activity. Complete the activity the day after you introduce the task. It can even be accomplished after the class completes Big6 #1, identifying the information needed to do the task.

1. Have each student write the task in his or her own words.
2. Read aloud and compare with others in the class (without commenting on others' interpretations).
3. Check for understanding by restating and displaying the task as summarized the day before.
4. Tell students to compare their interpretation to that which is displayed. Could they do this successfully as an independent assignment?
5. Have each student record the correct task. Tell them that knowing what to do is the first step toward success. (Jansen 75)

Works Cited

Jansen, Barbara A. *The Big6 in Middle School: Teaching Information and Communications Technology Skills*. Columbus, OH: Linworth Books, 2007.
Merriam-Webster's Collegiate Dictionary. 10th Edition, Springfield, MA: Merriam-Webster, Inc., 1995.

CHAPTER 5
Big6 #2 What Can We Use to Find What We Need?

Guiding Questions

- What are good sources of information for primary-age students?
- What strategies can help kindergartners through third graders choose appropriate sources?

Choosing the best sources to support an information search remains an elusive skill for primary students due to their developmental level and limited experiences with sources. The teacher and library media specialist will typically make the ultimate decision about best sources for particular needs. However, there are strategies you can employ to instill an awareness of selection in your students and to set them on the path of choosing best sources.

Introducing Strategies for Big6 #2 What Can We Use to Find What We Need?

Getting Started: Planning

Consider the reading level of your students. Most kindergartners and first graders are nonreaders or emerging readers, preventing them from reading from typical information sources. As new readers, second and third graders may still experience difficulty reading from most information sources. Even if some young children can "call words," they may not comprehend the facts and ideas in expository texts or be able to make connections to the needed information. However, some simple trade books, children's encyclopedias, and children's magazine articles may have appropriate vocabulary, allowing new readers to locate needed information.

Nonreaders, Emerging Readers, or Whole Class Activities

Information sources that older helpers will read to the whole class or groups of children can, of course, have more challenging vocabulary, and those helpers will explain the words as encountered in the reading. Select books and other print (including online) materials that contain large, color photographs and bright illustrations to keep the interest of the children as they listen to the text read aloud. Choose other sources of information in which nonreaders can interact: bring in guest speakers to talk about the topic and to answer children's questions; make email contact with high school subject-area classes; interview parents or grandparents; survey classmates and school personnel; use tactile materials for observation, such as real objects; show engaging videos; and take field trips that will allow for observation and hands-on experiences. Of course, these additional sources will excite and engage new readers, also.

New Readers

Many second graders and most third graders (and the occasional kindergartner and first grader) can and should begin to read simple texts for information. However, they are cognitively unable to select appropriate materials, due to their limited reading abilities, lack of experience, and inability to evaluate texts for accuracy and authority. With assistance from their teachers and library media specialist, they can begin to brainstorm sources and help identify those that are best. Teachers and library media specialists will take care to select those sources that answer needed questions and are on the appropriate reading level for the intended audience. Many children's subscription databases, such as *Searchasaurus* by EBSCOhost and *eLibrary Elementary* by ProQuest, offer reading levels for included articles, reference sources, and Web sites.

Delivering Instruction

Sing the Big6 #2 verse (with the puppet if you are using one, see Chapter 10) and have students sing the refrain. Ask students what will help them get answers to the questions they are interested in about their topic—those written for Big6 #1 *What do we need to do?* Record their brainstorming ideas and add to the list those sources you have identified during planning. Share the pen as appropriate (see Chapter 3).

Review each source on the list and talk to the class about its value to the topic. Circle the sources that:

- answer the questions determined in Big6 #1,
- are on an appropriate reading level if students will read independently for information,
- are readily accessible in the classroom or school library,
- engage the learners, and
- allow interaction from the students.

Additional Strategies for Big6 #2

Choosing between a Book and an Encyclopedia

New readers can begin to understand the difference in information presented in a book and an encyclopedia.

1. Prepare sentence strips containing simple ready-reference questions for an upcoming topic. For instance, if the class is searching for basic information on the countries from the Cinderella stories they read, include, "What language is spoken in India?" and "What type of money is used in China?" Gather children's books and encyclopedia volumes about the topic.

2. Put children in pairs (number each pair) and hand out sentence strips and either a book or an encyclopedia that will answer the question.

3. Talk about the differences between an encyclopedia article and a book about India.

4. Provide the following instructions for the class:

   a. Pick up the sentence and read the question.

   b. In the book or encyclopedia you have, find the answer to the question.

   c. When you find the answer, stand up and go to the front of the room.

5. As each pair comes to the front, write its group number on the board. After all or most groups have been to the front, focus the class's attention on the board. Call each group number and ask the pair which source they used—a book or an encyclopedia. Write this beside each pair's number. Students should see that the encyclopedias were almost always at the top half of the list.

6. Discuss using encyclopedias for many "ready-reference" questions, those questions that have a "right" answer—a fact. Books are useful for longer explanations and more detailed information on a topic. (Jansen, "Which is Best" 71)

Using the Process of Exclusion to Teach Second and Third Graders How to Develop a List of Sources

1. Cut notebook paper in half lengthwise and give a piece to each group of students.

2. Each group brainstorms and records possible resources that will contain answers to their questions. Suggest that students think of those found on library shelves as well as online.

3. The teacher or library media specialist uses the "Process of Exclusion" to record each group's list.

   a. The first group reads its entire list as the teacher writes the sources on an overhead transparency or other large display.

   b. Instruct the other groups to place checkmarks by any sources on their own lists that have been recorded on the display.

   c. The second group reads only those items that do not have a checkmark while other groups place checkmarks by those items on their list that the second group reads.

   d. Continue until all groups have read items that have no checkmarks.

   e. The teacher or library media specialist adds any sources to the list that the groups missed or those that he wants to introduce to the class.

4. Discuss the benefits and drawbacks of each source. Those that are not available or that will not meet the requirements of the task will be crossed off the list. Most likely students will have "Internet" or "Google" on their lists. Instead, tell students that they mean Web sites that contain information about their topic. Discuss with the students that Internet and search engines are not actual sources but ways of accessing content-related Web sites, therefore Big6 #3 *Location and Access* will be the step that helps them use the Internet and Google.

5. The teacher instructs each group to choose two to four sources from the overhead list that will best meet the needs of the task. (They may need to do this for each question being answered in the task, as not all resources will answer all questions.) Instruct each group to tell which ones it has chosen. Place checkmarks beside each resource on the overhead as it is chosen. The ones with the most checkmarks will most likely be the resources that will be used for that assignment. The teacher may direct groups to include particular sources—especially if he is introducing new or unknown resources to the class. Consider allowing individual groups to add resources of their own with your approval, as some students may have additional access.

6. Direct students' attention to the projected Big6 chart or poster. Tell them that they have completed both parts of Big6 #2 *Information Seeking Strategies*—brainstorm all possible sources and select the best sources. (Jansen, "What Can I Use" 69)

Instruct students to record the sources in their Big6 Research Journal (see Appendix E). The benefits of using the process of exclusion to introduce step 2 of the process to students include 1) requiring students to listen to each other to avoid repetition when sharing results of brainstorming; 2) allowing the teacher to introduce new or previously unknown resources to students; 3) giving the teacher direction on where to begin or review instruction in accessing and using general or specific resources; and 4) giving students a focus for engaging in the assignment, so they have a place to start and other resources to consult if the computer stations are in use!

Awareness of Web Evaluation

While early learners' cognitive abilities and levels of experience keep them from being able to evaluate a Web site for accuracy and authority, the teacher or library media specialist can instill a sense of awareness. Some educators place Web evaluation in Big6 #4 *Use of Information—What information can we use?* Whether or not you present Web evaluation in Big6 #2 or in #4, the most important concern is that it IS presented to students. Take a few minutes before children use a Web site to talk about the reasons you chose it for their use. Consider using Diane Lauer's "5Ws of Web Site Evaluation" <http://dianelauer.com/fivewww/webeval.html> to structure the discussion. Display a Web site and discuss the following points:

- **Who** wrote the pages and are they an expert in the field?
- **What** is the purpose of the site? (To inform or educate, to entertain, to sell, to persuade, to communicate)
- **Where** does the information come from?
- **When** was the site created, updated, or last worked on? (And why is this important?)
- **Why** is the information valuable? (Lauer)

Works Cited

Jansen, Barbara A. *The Big6 in Middle School: Teaching Information and Communications Technology Skills.* Columbus, OH: Linworth Books, Inc., 2007.

_____. "What Can I Use for This Project? Teaching Students to Select Sources." *Teaching Information and Technology Skills: The Big6 in Elementary Schools.* By Michael B. Eisenberg and Robert E. Berkowitz. Worthington, OH: Linworth Publishing, Inc, 1999.

_____. "Which is Best? Choosing the Resource for Me." *Teaching Information and Technology Skills: The Big6 in Elementary Schools.* By Michael B. Eisenberg and Robert E. Berkowitz. Worthington, OH: Linworth Publishing, Inc, 1999.

Lauer, Diane. "The Five W's of Web Site Evaluation: A Primer for Teachers and Students." *Diane Lauer.* 9 Nov. 1999. 21 Nov. 2008 <http://dianelauer.com/?fivewww/?webeval.html>.

CHAPTER 6
Big6 #3 Where Can We Find What We Need?

Guiding Questions

- What strategies will give nonreaders and emerging readers an awareness of locating sources and accessing the information within?
- What strategies can help new readers locate sources?
- How can new readers access information within sources?

For young learners, one of the most difficult stages of the information search process is that of locating sources and the information contained within. Nonreaders and emerging readers will depend on their teacher or library media specialist to bring the source to the whole group, while the Big6 Buddy (see introduction to Part 3) will deliver the sources of information to small groups. New readers will begin to locate their own sources with much adult supervision and help.

Introducing Strategies for Big6 #3
Where Can We Find What We Need?
Getting Started: Planning

Is this a whole class or small group project? If it is whole class, you will locate the materials for the class. If students are working in small groups, put materials on reserve or create Information Stations as explained in the next section. Big6 Buddies may also locate materials for their Little Buddies.

Delivering Instruction

Sing the Big6 #3 verse (with the puppet if you are using one, see Chapter 10) and have students sing the refrain. *Whole group (class) project*: Tell or demonstrate to the class the steps used to locate the book or other material used for the search. *Small group project:* Demonstrate to the groups how the materials were selected for the reserve shelf or the Information Stations.

Additional Strategies for Big6 #3
Locating Sources for Nonreaders and Emerging Readers

Even the youngest learners can select a book from a cart, provided it has a picture of their topic on the cover. For students working individually or in small groups with Big6 Buddies, place appropriate books on a cart or table. Once you assign or students choose a topic, pull accompanying books from classroom and library book shelves and place them on a cart or table. Students can then find the appropriate book based on the illustration or photograph on the cover. This works especially well with books about specific animals or animal groups.

Information Stations

An efficient way to organize sources that students will use, whether or not they will work with a Big6 Buddy, is to create "information stations" throughout the library or classroom. Label each station with a colorful sign and simple directions for the learners (see Figure 6.1). The teacher or library media specialist can instruct the class in the use of each station. However, too many instructions at once may overwhelm students. If groups are with Big6 Buddies, those older helpers can go over the instructions as they visit each station. Second semester second graders and third graders may be able to use stations independently or in small groups. The teacher, library media specialist, and any other available adult can assist as needed.

Figure 6.1 Information Station Sign

THIS COMPUTER
has
Britannica Online

1. Type your topic in the search box.

SEARCH [TREE FROG]

2. Click (GO▶)
3. Put the red cup on top if you need help.

Considerations: Even though computer stations are capable of accessing multiple resources, designate one source per computer and label it appropriately. Have the source ready to use. Instruct the users to leave the source open when they exit the station and to click the source's "home" button to leave it ready for the next user. Place a colorful plastic cup upside down at each station. Instruct students to place it on top of their computer if they need help.

Have as many stations as you have sets of encyclopedias. Place each set on its own table or, if you do not wish to remove the sets from the shelf, put each title (*World Book, New Book of Knowledge, Encyclopedia of Animals*, etc.) on individual tables so students know where to sit and use that particular encyclopedia title. This will alleviate crowding and confusion around the encyclopedia shelf and help direct the correct re-shelving of volumes.

Rotate each group through the stations in an orderly manner so that all groups get to use each station. Allow 15-20 minutes (depending on learners and engagement) at each station. The information gathering may take several periods spread out over two to three days.

Using Children's Subscription Databases

Many school libraries have access to databases targeted at the upper elementary age group: Gale's *Kids InfoBits,* NewsBank *KidsPage,* EBSCOhost *Searchasaurus,* SIRS *Discoverer*, and ProQuest's *eLibrary Elementary* to name a few. While these databases offer safe searching and subject directories, results can still be overwhelming in number and difficult to navigate. Be cautious when turning students loose to search at will; the numerous hits and many links can confuse and frustrate even the brightest students, and many of the irrelevant returns can waste precious class time. How then, do you maximize the potential power of these databases and use class time efficiently? Do your homework! Spend some time exploring the best search terms for the upcoming topics and anticipate how your students will use the search features. Try several searches, see how the results change, and judge the effectiveness of your searches. If students do their own searching under your supervision, you will need to be fairly direct in guiding them to the most effective search terms and word combinations.

Locating Sites on the Free Web

Children love the Internet and feel empowered when using it. The varied skills needed to successfully use a search engine such as Google or Yahoo are out of the scope of what a young learner can accomplish. Instead, searching or browsing a subject directory may be within the reach of a new reader. Professional educators or editors have chosen the Web sites included in these collections. Consider using a children's subject directory such as *KidsClick* <http://kidsclick.org> or American Library Association's *Great Web Sites for Kids* <http://ala.org/gwstemplate.cfm?section=greatwebsites&template=/

cfapps/gws/default.cfm>, as they employ a selection criteria, including sites that meet a high standard. Before you introduce a subject directory to the class, perform several searches and browse the collection to see what results students will most likely get. In addition, check to see if your school or district purchased a subscription to a subject directory of free Web sites such as *netTrekker* <http://nettrekker.com> or *WebFeet* <http://gale.cengage.com/webfeet/>.

More Ideas for Locating Sources

Young children can learn which sections of the school library contain nonfiction and reference materials (see Chapter 12).

- Due to limited time for research and students' undeveloped skill level in locating sources, putting materials on reserve and making links available is a viable alternative to having students locate these resources independently. With the location step of the process done for the students, more time can be spent on teaching skills needed to access information within the source. When providing links and putting library materials on physical reserve, consider modeling how you located those materials (Jansen 29).

- Second graders should begin to locate encyclopedia articles by the first letter of the volume. They will need help, however, locating and reading the specific article within the volume. Considering their reading abilities, using the index may be developmentally out of reach.

- Independent use of the library's online catalog may be too difficult for kindergartners and first graders. Successful use depends on accurate spelling and the ability to understand author, title, and subject. In addition, students must be able to locate the books on the shelf. The school library media specialist has appropriate activities to instruct these early learners in the arrangement of the library before they are introduced to its online or card catalog.

- Second graders are usually ready for the library's catalog, especially by the second half of the year. As their spelling may be inaccurate, they should be instructed to bring a piece of paper and pencil to an adult in the library for correct spelling. Keep supplies by the terminals. The library media specialist has engaging activities to teach students how to use the online (or card) catalog.

Accessing an Article within an Encyclopedia Volume

Use this activity to teach ready students how to quickly access the correct part of the encyclopedia volume to save time finding an article.

1. Each pair or group of second or third grade students looks at their topic (for example, a planet name such as Saturn) and gets the appropriate encyclopedia. Use a graphic (Figure 6.2) to show how to select the correct volume if there is more than one for a single letter (sometimes the S, for example, is in two volumes: S-Sn and So-Sz).

Figure 6.2 Choosing the Correct Encyclopedia Volume

2. Show a transparency of the alphabet letters and have students identify the second letter of their topic name. They should write the topic and circle the second letter—check for spelling. Using a transparency pen, divide the alphabet into thirds. Have the students choose the part (beginning, middle, or end) of the alphabet where the second letter falls. Demonstrate the process for the students using a topic similar to theirs. For example, if studying the planets, choose Pluto (since it is no longer classified as a planet, but will have an entry in the encyclopedia). Demonstrate how the "l" is in the middle of the encyclopedia so that is where you will open it.

3. Tell students that they should open the volume to the beginning, middle, or end of the encyclopedia before looking for the exact page on which the article is located. This will save a lot of time, instead of paging through the entire volume if the topic is toward the middle or end. Have students practice with several topics if needed. Repeat the instruction for each information search.

4. Find the exact article and mark it with a sticky note. Mark the end of the article with a second sticky note.

Identifying Keywords and Related Words

Due to the varied terminology and vocabulary used, many new readers have difficulty making the connection between the information needed and the information presented in a book or online. The students' natural language (as written in the questions they developed in Big6 #1) will certainly differ from the language in a source. Students' limited vocabulary and experience with reading for information may impede their efforts in finding relevant information. This exercise "unlocks" the meaning in the sentence and provides additional access points.

1. Display a question written in Big6 #1, such as "What are the state's natural resources?" The teacher or library media specialist explains the terms "keyword" or "key phrase." Ask "What is this question really asking?" and then underline the important word or words (ex. What are the state's <u>natural resources</u>?).

2. Have each student or groups of students look at the questions they wrote for Big6 #1 and direct them to underline the important words (keywords or phrases) in each question. Once students understand what is required, this process seems simple.

3. Demonstrate writing related words beside or under the keywords on the sample question:

    a. Ex. What are the state's <u>natural resources</u>? = rivers, lakes, other water sources, land use—agriculture and cattle grazing, wildlife, native trees, and other plants

    b. Ex. What are the <u>famous landmarks</u> in the state? = mountains, hill country, rivers, lakes, famous buildings and cemeteries, monuments, other structures

4. Students should write related words beside or under the keywords. The teacher or library media specialist will check students' work and give suggestions as needed, due to the students' limited vocabulary.

5. Tell students that they will look for the keywords and related words when they are searching for information in a source, such as in the table of contents, index, and other features.

Using the Structure of Expository Texts (Essential Points of Access) to Find Information within a Source

Entering text at point of need and exiting with the needed information remains a difficult task for even middle and high school students. New readers will greatly benefit by learning the organization of expository texts as they begin to read for information. Most students learn to read from narrative texts—the telling of a story. The story has a beginning, a middle, and an end. The entire story must usually be read to comprehend the full meaning. Expository texts vary greatly from this structure. When used for information searching, the reader should *not* read the entire text, as this would waste time.

Understanding the structure of expository texts goes a long way in helping a new reader enter the text at point of need. The main features of expository texts (or essential points of access) include table of contents, index, and glossary. Other essential points of access, which are used more extensively in Big6 #4 *What information can I use?,* are titles and subtitles; headings and subheadings; topic sentences; section titles and labels; captions for photographs and illustrations; graphics and icons; tabs and links—whatever is appropriate for that page.

Nonreaders, emerging readers, and whole class instruction:
Kindergartners and first graders can begin to gain an awareness of these features from their teacher and library media specialist as they are reading aloud. Point out the table of contents and read the chapter headings. Ask which chapter might have information about the topic or question. Show the index and tell the students that it helps find specific information within chapters.

New readers (grades 2 and 3) should begin to use tables of content and indices to find information within sources. Begin instruction using students' social studies or science textbooks. Explain that chapter headings are like a main idea for the content included in the corresponding chapter and the index lists supporting details. Give students a topic and ask in which chapter they will most likely find it. Turn to the index, give words to find, and have them tell corresponding page numbers. When students write books about themselves, have them include a table of contents and an index.

Navigating a Web Page

If educators allow new readers to use Web pages for information, they must teach students how to navigate the pages. Most Web pages contain multiple links to other pages within that Web site or to completely different Web sites. Teach students to read or look at the entire page or section first. Then if they need additional information, they should click on the appropriate link. Typically, links do not further explain a word or concept, but take the user to a page that has similar or additional information, sometimes not even related. If students click on links before they finish reading, their train of thought is interrupted and it will be difficult to refocus even if they do get back to the original page.

While advertisers sponsor a site, instruct children to refrain from clicking on the advertisements, because this is just one more distraction as it will open multiple pop-up pages or take the student to a completely different site.

Works Cited

Jansen, Barbara A. "Relieving the Confusion: Location and Access Made (Relatively) Easy." *Library Media Connection*, April/May 2005.

CHAPTER 7
Big6 #4 What Information Can We Use?

Guiding Questions

- How can young learners engage in the source?
- What strategies can help nonreaders and emerging readers take notes?
- How can new readers take notes effectively?
- Which organizers can help primary students systematically take notes?
- How can young learners give credit to sources at point of use?

When educators of intermediate and older students who have used the Big6 for years think of Big6 #4 *Use of Information,* what comes to mind is reading and taking notes. Experienced teachers of primary-age children know that reading expository texts, extracting needed information, and recording that information in a systematic manner may be out of the reach of their young students. Much depends on successful note taking in the early grades. Kindergartners, most first, and many second graders will not have the developmental readiness to read and take notes independently. Many third graders will struggle with this skill, needing individual help. Careful educators will assess the readiness of their students and plan so that all students succeed in taking essential information from the source.

Introducing Strategies for Big6 #4
What Information Can We Use?

Getting Started: Planning

Consider these questions as you plan to help children engage in the source and extract needed information:

1. How will the class be grouped—whole group, small groups, individual students? (Occasionally, having only a single copy of a source may dictate whole class activities.)

2. What is the source of information? (Book, online source, video or audio recording, real object)

3. Who is responsible for reading—the teacher or library media specialist, Big6 Buddies, or the students?

4. Who is responsible for recording needed information (taking notes)—the teacher or library media specialist, Big6 Buddies, or the students?

5. On what type of organizer will the note taker record information?

6. How will we cite sources at point of use?

Delivering Instruction

Sing the Big6 #4 verse (with the puppet if you are using one, see Chapter 10) and have students sing the refrain. Depending on the student grouping and source of information used, implement the appropriate strategy (see Additional Strategies section) for engaging in the source and extracting the information needed as determined in Big6 #1. If using puppets, have fun with the children and forget inhibitions—puppets are a powerful way to engage children in information.

Look at the grouping for students as determined in the planning. In the next sections you will find the appropriate note-taking method and organizer as determined by the class grouping. Take care to select developmentally appropriate strategies for your students.

Additional Strategies for Big6 #4

Teaching Observation Skills for Recording Notes from Objects

When using real objects from the manufactured or natural world, children should use as many senses as appropriate to describe the items in terms of the information need as determined in Big6 #1. Try this activity to jump start their powers of observation.

1. Collect various small rocks and distribute one to each child. Tell the children to wait for your instructions before touching the rocks, which is their natural tendency. As children answer the questions about the rock, record their responses on a large display.

2. Ask students to watch the rock. What does it do? Listen to it. Does it make a sound? How can they describe its shape? Its color? Can they predict how much it weighs (don't pick it up!)? Does it weigh more or less than this book (hold up a book)? More or less than a piece of paper (show a sheet of paper)?

3. Now pick it up. Turn it over in your hands. How does it feel? What words can you use to describe its texture? Drop it on your desk (or floor if students are in a group on the carpet). What sound does it make? Smell your rock. What words can you use to describe the way it smells?

4. You just observed your rock. What does observing mean?

5. Repeat this activity frequently, changing the object that the children observe. Eventually, have different students ask the questions until all students have taken a turn.

6. When children are fairly proficient at observing, have them help you make an Observation Chart for the classroom to which they will refer when using real objects in Big6 #4 (see Figure 7.1).

Figure 7.1 Sample Observation Chart

Observation Chart	
What is the object?	**How does the object look?**
How does the object feel?	**How does the object smell?**
How does the object sound?	**What else can I observe about the object?**

Listening with a Purpose: Reading Aloud to Young Children from Books and Online Sources Using the Collaborative Note Taking Method

When taking notes for a whole class activity during a read aloud session, collaboration between the library media specialist and teacher will help students focus on the activity. Of course, it can be accomplished with one adult doing both the reading and recording. The students' role is that of critical listeners as they gain an awareness of using parts of the text instead of consuming all of it as they do with a story.

1. Have the class listen for the information defined in Big6 #1 as the teacher or library media specialist reads from an expository text. Start with one source, appropriately increasing to two or more as the year progresses.

2. Before beginning to read the appropriate section, review Big6 #3 and talk about the table of contents, directing students to figure out which chapter or section will answer a specific question. Turn to that page or section and begin to read. Students should identify the information needed by raising their hands or calling attention to the relevant passage in some way.

3. The relevant information is recorded in the student's own words if possible. Record on a chart tablet or other large display, with students sharing the pen as often as possible (see Chapter 3).

4. Cite the source (in a simple fashion) and explain what you are doing and the importance of giving credit to others' work.

Figure 7.2 Collaborative Note Taking

Adult A reads sections containing "answers" to pre-determined question(s)

Students listen critically for "answers" to question(s)

Adult B scribes notes on chart tablet or board for students to use in Big6 #5

Viewing and Listening with a Purpose: Using Video and Audio Recordings

Children watch television passively—all input and no output. They acquire this habit early in life because the television is mesmerizing and seems to magically hold their attention. Most children watch intently with little physical movement in their eyes or bodies since most programs require no interaction. Viewing video or listening to audio recordings for a purpose other than to entertain requires skills not learned by watching television. Many educators allow passive viewing of instructional video and audio recordings. Simple strategies employed by the teacher will turn children from a passive consumers of the content to critical contributors to their learning.

1. Preview the video or audio recording to ensure that it will answer questions posed in Big6 #1 and that it is developmentally appropriate.

2. Prior to playing the recording, review the questions the class wrote in Big6 #1. Tell students that they will listen for answers to those questions. You can divide the class into groups and assign one question per group so not to overwhelm and confuse the students. Tell students to raise their hand when they hear the answers to their question.

3. Play the recording, pausing as students raise hands. If no student raises a hand, pause and repeat the script that answered a question. Ask, "Which question did that answer?" If no student answers, rewind and play again or simply tell the question that it answered.

4. Record the answer to the question.

5. Repeat step 3 until the recording ends.

6. After several sessions of active listening and viewing, students will become more proficient. Young learners will not master this skill but will increase their awareness of purposeful engagement.

Taking Notes with Big6 Buddies

Note taking with a Big6 Buddy (see Introduction to Part 3) works best with small groups or individual students who are not able to take their own notes or when the teacher wants small groups or individuals to study subtopics of a larger unit. For instance in the study of dental health, students may be divided into groups to study one of the following topics: tooth brushing, visiting the dentist, healthy eating, and safe play. Have older students or parent helpers (see the introduction to Part 3) help the younger students locate their specific information as defined in Big6 #1. Big6 Buddies should tell the younger students what they are doing each step of the way and show or explain how they take notes. If possible, the younger students will listen as the Big6 Buddy reads aloud the relevant passage. The younger student should identify the correct "answer," and the Buddy should record it in the words of the younger student or explain it in a simplified way that the younger student can understand before recording. Big6 Buddies may share the pen (see Chapter 3) if instructed in that strategy. Use any of the note-taking organizers below as appropriate. If the younger student does not identify the relevant information, the Buddy should stop and explain why that is the "correct answer."

Learning from Guest Speakers

When engaging the services of a guest speaker, consider giving them the children's questions in preparation for the visit. Talk to the speaker about how you will record the presentation by hand or using a tape or video recorder. Some speakers may allow themselves to be recorded for later playback. However, you will need to obtain the speaker's permission. During the presentation or talk, he or she can include the "answers" to the questions in the talk or allow children to ask the questions. The speaker should emphasize important points and allow the teacher time to record them on a large display if he is not being electronically recorded. Or, the speaker can write the important notes on the board for students to record after the talk. Employ the strategy in the previous section for taking notes during the playback of the audio or video recording of the speaker.

Taking Notes the Trash and Treasure Way

New readers are ready to begin taking factual notes, recording words and phrases from sources. Using the "trash and treasure" method to instruct some second graders and third graders helps students identify the needed sections of a reference source and also specific words to extract for their stated purpose.

Direct instruction is necessary the first few times students are required to take notes for an assignment. While new readers will not become independent users of the process, frequent review helps reinforce the concept of not copying needless information from a source. Relate note taking to a pirate's treasure map (show one if necessary—a Google search will return a number of treasure maps, or you may draw a rough one). You may have to explain the use of treasure maps in the days of pirates and train/stagecoach robbers. The map itself is like the article or chapter of a book containing information about the topic. The X on the map, which marks the exact location of the buried treasure, is the section of the text containing needed information or "answers" for specific questions defined in *Task Definition*. A pirate or treasure hunter must dig for the chest, shoveling aside "trash"—dirt, weeds, and rocks. A researcher must dig to find the "treasure"—words that help answer the questions. He or she must "shovel aside" unnecessary sentences, phrases, and words we do not need (trash words). Of course, these words are not trash to the original source, only to the researcher, because they do not answer the questions defined in the task. Ask students to help you act out digging for treasure. Demonstrate this concept using a projected image of an encyclopedia article or section. The students should each have a copy of the article so they can follow along and practice the technique.

1. Show a prepared question, including the underlined keywords and list of related words.

2. Skim the article for essential points of access (titles and subtitles; headings and subheadings; topic sentences; section titles and labels; captions for photographs and illustrations; graphics and icons; tabs and links) until you locate the appropriate place in the document.

3. Place a slash at the end of the first sentence and read it. Ask "Does this sentence answer the question?"

4. If the answer is no, tell the students that this sentence is "trash" to them. Go on to the next sentence, placing a slash at the end.

5. If the answer is yes, underline the first phrase and ask if that phrase answers the question. If the answer is no, underline the next phrase and repeat the question.

6. If the answer is yes, read that phrase word by word, asking which words are needed to answer the question—treasure words. Circle those words, then write them in the appropriate place on the projected data chart or whichever organizer the students are using. Those that do not answer the question are trash words. Continue phrase by phrase and word by word until the end of the sentence. Count the words in the sentence and then count the treasure words. Students are very impressed when you say, "The sentence has 17 words and I only needed to write four of them. I don't know about you, but I would rather write four than 17!"

7. Demonstrate the process again on another sentence, allowing the students to practice using copies of the article. Students should practice independently a few times before they begin their own research. The library media specialist and teacher should monitor each student's work, re-teaching as necessary.

Once students understand the concept of "trash and treasure" words, they begin to write fewer and fewer unnecessary words while note taking. (Jansen 109-10)

Note Taking Organizers

Word Wall

Commonly used in primary classrooms, the word wall acts as a record of new vocabulary encountered during instructional units and other discussions in the classroom. A word wall is typically specific to an instructional unit so that students can scaffold and categorize new words. During a read aloud session for a whole group unit, post a large bulletin board or piece of paper so that it is easily accessible by the teacher or students who are sharing the pen. Add new words as encountered in the study of a topic. The teacher can cite the source below the words to give children an awareness of attribution. (See Figure 7.3). Once finished with the reading and discussion, kindergartners and first graders can use the words to write what they remember or have taken an interest in about the topic. Some first graders and second graders can use the words to write notes that answer specific questions.

Figure 7.3 Word Wall

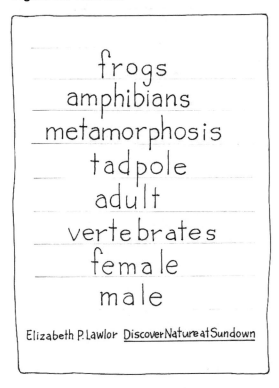

frogs
amphibians
metamorphosis
tadpole
adult
vertebrates
female
male

Elizabeth P. Lawlor Discover Nature at Sundown

Data Chart

Second and third graders can use a data chart for recording factual notes
(Figure 7.4). Younger students, with the help of Big6 Buddies, can successfully
use it also. It keeps all notes from all sources together on one page, which may
be considered a drawback if children need to reorganize or categorize notes in
Big6 #5 *How can we show what we learned?* However, most young students do
not need to reorganize notes. Each student folds a piece of large white drawing
paper into 16 boxes. The creases form the borders of the boxes. (Teachers can
create a similar effect by inserting a table in a word processor using landscape
view, with four columns and four rows. However, using standard paper creates
very small boxes for recording notes.) Students record notes for knowledge-level
information in the appropriate boxes. There is enough space for them to answer
seven questions (three on front and four on back). If they have more to answer,
you may want to re-think the number or use a different note taking organizer.

Figure 7.4 Data Chart

My name: My topic:	Question #1	Question #2	Question #3
Source #1			
Source #2			
Source #3 or summary			

Note Taking Boxes

Second graders whose information needs include only three or four questions can easily fold one piece of drawing paper into fourths (see Figure 7.5). At the top of each box, students write one question leaving space to record "answers" and draw pictures. On the back or at the bottom of the sheet, the child will cite the source or sources used.

Figure 7.5 Note Taking Boxes

Draw an outline of the country's map.	Draw the country's flag.
What language do most people speak?	**What types of food do the people eat?**

Note Taking Folder

A third grade teacher at Live Oak Elementary in Austin, Texas, handed out research folders for each group. In the file folder, she directed students to staple one sandwich bag in which to keep "snip-its," small squares of paper, similar to note cards, on which students kept factual bits of information. In addition, she instructed students to staple one page of notebook paper to the other side on which they cited their sources. They numbered each source and wrote the corresponding number on each "snip-it." Students also kept track of drafts, sketches, and final work in the folder. Students stored the folders in a central place in the classroom for easy access.

Note Taking Using Kidspiration

When the teacher or students create a bubble organizer in the children's software program Kidspiration (see Figure 4.2), the program allows them to take notes by clicking on the "Go to Writing" icon at the bottom of the window. The subtopics (questions) appear on a writing tablet page, allowing for note taking (see Figure 7.6). The teacher or capable students can easily record notes and send them to a Microsoft Word, plain text, or AppleWorks file for further editing or inclusion in a report or other document. It is on the word processing page that students can cite their sources. Very young students can, with a Big6 Buddy, use the record feature and talk about what they see in photographs, real objects, and illustrations.

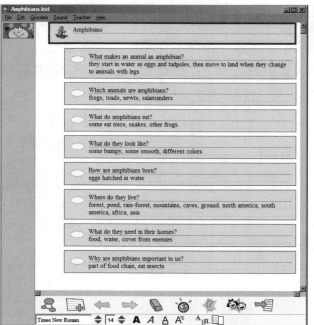

Figure 7.6

Note Taking Boxes in Kidspiration

©2007 Inspiration Software®, Inc. Diagram created in Kidspiration® by Inspiration Software®, Inc. Used with permission.

Citing Sources at Point of Use

Teaching children to cite sources at point of use (Big6 #4) and again in a formal bibliography (Big6 #5) will go a long way in preventing plagiarism in later years. Begin by recording the title and author of any source used by the teacher or student during note taking. At this age, teachers and students do not need to employ formal citation standards such as those published by the Modern Language Association or the American Psychological Association. Simply noting the author and title adequately gives attribution. Cite the source on the note taking organizer when recording notes. Explain to students the reason for giving attribution or "thanks" when taking notes.

Works Cited

Jansen, Barbara A. *The Big6 in Middle School: Teaching Information and Communications Technology Skills*. Columbus, OH: Linworth Books, 2007.

CHAPTER 8
Big6 #5 How Can We Show What We Learned?

Guiding Questions

- How can young learners organize information found in sources?
- How can primary students show the results of the information search as they learn transferable skills?
- What strategies can help young learners "go beyond" the information in sources by adding original ideas and thinking on a higher level?
- How can young learners understand the concept of copyright and plagiarism?
- How will young students give credit to their sources by organizing a simple bibliography?
- What audience will children have for their efforts?

Introducing Strategies for Big6 #5
How Can We Show What We Learned?

Getting Started: Planning

When creating a final product, young students can and should do more than simply copy the facts found in sources. By setting high expectations, children can think about the information they found on a higher level than it was originally presented in the source. Alongside crediting sources, higher-level thinking also helps to prevent deliberate or accidental plagiarism in later years because students learn not to merely copy-and-paste from sources for the requirements of the assignment.

When planning activities, consider that very young students may not be developmentally ready to construct group products, but they can add an individual offering to a class project. For example, each student contributes a page to a class book. When students are ready to cooperate in small groups to create the final product, a group effort produces interesting outcomes and collaborative products. However, for accurate assessment, each child should also complete an individual product, either written or oral, in order to determine if the student understands main concepts and skills.

Decide on the best product for the child to show what he or she learned. Gather and prepare the materials as needed. Consider collaborating with the school's technologist to teach developmentally appropriate technology skills if using children's productivity software such as KidPix.

Delivering Instruction

Sing the Big6 #5 verse (with the puppet if you are using one, see Chapter 10) and have students sing the refrain. Tell them that Big6 #5 *How can we show what we learned?* will help them put their information together. It is important that they organize their ideas and information before they create the final product. Demonstrate to the students the way they will organize their information. For example, show how they will assemble a booklet before actually stapling, taping, or gluing. Then provide them with an example of the final product, as visualizing may be difficult for very young students. Give clear expectations and directions, repeating as necessary as you monitor each student's progress.

Additional Strategies and Considerations for Big6 #5

Simple Ideas for Showing Results

Individual Booklet

For very young children, teachers will cut out the pieces of the book and demonstrate its assembly. Children illustrate the pages with the information they found. In Figure 8.1, each page has one spider fact and on the last page, the student tells why he thinks spiders are important.

Second and third graders can use Microsoft PowerPoint to construct and print a book. They can use the features of PowerPoint to add facts and original ideas about their topic. Students can illustrate their book with clip art, photos or illustrations from online sources, or original art created using a paint

program such as KidPix or the drawing
tools in Microsoft Word. When each
page (slide) is completed, printing and
stapling the slides make a nice booklet.
Instruct children to include their
sources and an About the Author
section on the last slides.

Figure 8.1 Individual Spider Booklet

Class Book

All students can contribute a page for a
class book. The teacher can help the
class construct a cover, title page, table of contents, and page of sources. Ask
the library media specialist to catalog or mark it for checkout in the library.

Oral Presentations

All state academic standards require children to recite or speak orally.
Providing opportunities at an early age will help them perform with ease by
the time they reach high school and beyond. Children can tell all they know
about their topic. Then teachers can ask specific questions about the topic and
add those questions that require original thought and higher-level thinking.

Children in second and third grades can write and perform simple skits about
their topics. They can read aloud original stories or poems about their topic
using the Big6 (see Chapter 11).

Showing Results While Learning Transferable Skills

Consider which transferable skills students will learn as they add value to the
final product. Transferable skills include:

- Composition
- Technology
- Production
- Performance
- Presentation

Of course, you do not need to include all skills every time, but an effective
combination may include writing and performing a script or illustrating an
original story using KidPix software. However, consider including a composition
(story, letter, poem, or a few sentences) each time students engage in the
information search process, even if students dictate their ideas. When each
student produces a composition, you can more easily assess specific skills and
content the student gained from the experience, along with providing
opportunities for students to write in various subject areas. Students can complete
group projects concurrently with the individually written response using many

forms of creative expression that result in a presentation, performance, or production using a variety of technology applications when appropriate.

Collaborating with teachers in other subject areas and the technology department, as appropriate, to aid students in synthesizing information adds another dimension to the learning: students see a dynamic team of experts working together on their behalf. The library media specialist, homeroom teacher, language arts, fine arts, and technology specialists planning and teaching in tandem, for example, integrates a number of transferable skills taught at a level any one teacher may not be able to reach alone.

Primary students can effectively collaborate on group products; however, each student should also provide evidence of his or her knowledge and understandings of concepts and skills through writing compositions such as stories or reports that include information from consulting sources as well as evidence of higher-level thought.

Most state curriculum standards include using technology to show the results of an information search process or inquiry. Care must be taken not to design instruction using technology for technology's sake (see Chapter 2). If the nature of the final product allows meaningful use of technology, how can students effectively use the available technological resources to show results of information searching? What instruction do students need in using a specific technology? Is the technology use developmentally appropriate? Who will provide the instruction? Do you need to reserve a lab or laptop cart for several days in a row?

Going Beyond Information Found in Sources

Getting students to process the facts and other information they find using higher-level thought and original ideas will result in a final product that represents the best of what that student can offer. It will stretch a student's intellect and engage her in the learning process. When she adds personal value to the results, she takes more ownership and pride in her work. Going beyond the facts means that a student will have to use higher level skills to process the information found in sources instead of just rewriting or copying-and-pasting those facts into a report or other product.

How would higher-level thinking look in a final project to a kindergartner or first grader? Eliciting opinions from the youngest students to respond to questions such as "Why do you think...?" or "What might happen...?" begins teaching children that their ideas matter in the educational system. For example, questions can lead students to think about their civic and environmental responsibilities: "Why do you think we should not kill all spiders?" "What might happen if we didn't try to save some of the trees in our city?"

How would a second or third grader show higher-level thinking or original ideas? As students move from the preoperational level of cognitive development into the operational stage, teachers can ask a greater array of challenging questions and assignment components. For example, when studying the solar system ask a second grader how one would dress if visiting a certain planet. Comparing their lives to those of people who lived around 1492 escalates their thought process to a higher level. Add, "If your family had to travel back to 1492 to live for awhile, what do you have now that you would miss the most? Why?" Third graders can come up with a real or fictitious company that could benefit from a state's natural resources and try to persuade the company to relocate in their state. They can also ponder why a state's natural resources should or should not be consumed.

Asking questions from a variety of levels and expecting thoughtful responses will help children go beyond the information found in sources. Consider asking questions from the convergent, divergent, and evaluative levels for young students to think about when putting their information together (Ciardiello). See the *Big6 Kids* Web site for examples of questions to ask <www.big6.com/kids/site/category/grades-3-6/know-how-grades-3-6/>, based on fact, why, idea, and opinion questions.

Understanding Copyright and Plagiarism

While copyright and plagiarism are difficult and abstract concepts for even middle school students to understand, it is in elementary school that students innocently learn the bad habits of copying directly from a source without crediting. Even if the information they copy may be common knowledge and not need an in-text citation, young students are not capable of making that determination and need to credit all sources. Introducing young students to the concept of plagiarism will go a long way in preventing deliberate plagiarism in later years. Without scaring students or telling of the horrors of getting caught plagiarizing, library media specialists and teachers can talk about borrowing or taking a friend's toy without asking. Acting out the scenario, with and without asking permission, helps young learners visualize the deed and empathize with the owner. Tell students that using someone else's ideas from a book or Web site must be credited and sometimes they even need to ask permission. Usually, just giving credit will do.

Giving Credit to Sources

Compiling a bibliography, whether or not the student speaks, constructs, performs, or composes the final product, teaches an additional transferable skill and helps students avoid accidental plagiarism in later years. If students cite sources in Big6 #4 (see Chapter 7), they can, with help, put them in order for the bibliography.

Teachers of the youngest students can help them record the author and title of sources used to make an alphabetized bibliography. A mouthful, the word *bibliography,* has no meaning to the youngest learners so a library media specialist in Lumberton, Texas, tells her students that they will make a "Thank You" list of sources used.

With help, students in grades 2 and 3 can begin to alphabetize and add publication information as appropriate to their bibliographies. A formal MLA or APA citation is not usually necessary in the early grades—students need only understand that they give credit for all sources they use. If the product will be published and have a wider audience, the teacher may want to help students prepare a standard bibliography.

Providing an Audience for Student Efforts

Students will take more pride in work that will be viewed by many eyes, even if the "eyes" are imaginary, such as those in the third grade example lesson in Chapter 10. Or, knowing that the library will display their projects, students understand that any library visitor will view their work. You get the idea: stated audience = better results.

Works Cited

Ciardiello, Angelo V. "Did You Ask a Good Question Today? Alternative Cognitive and Metacognitive Strategies." *Journal of Adolescent and Adult Literacy* 42.3 (Nov. 1998): 210-219. *Professional Development Collection.* EBSCOhost. 2 Feb. 2000 <http://web.ebscohost.com/ehost/>.

CHAPTER 9
Big6 #6 How Will We Know If We Did Well?

Guiding Questions

- How can primary age children evaluate their efforts?
- Which questions will help young learners to think about their learning?

"Thank (think) hardor and eoos (use) the lidare (library) a lot mor."

—*Billy Jo, first grade*

"(Amphibians) are sometimes difrint to us. They think we are relley difrint to them. If they can think. (The Big6) relley helps us lern about stuff. Its a relley fin way to lern to."

—*Juana, first grade*

"I learned that the big 6 can help me find infarmatsion."

–*Dion, first grade*

"I lrnd that amphyibian have backbone. I lrnd that the Big Six holps you lorn."

—*Jordyn, first grade*

"I leared that using the Big 6 can help you a hole lot. I learned that sometimes you may need help because it can be hard. We lared (learned) a lot in the librery!'"

——*Mackenzie-Ann, second grade*

"I learnd that using a partner could really help on our brochure. I(f) my partner and me didn' get help from the (Big6 Buddies) then if I didn't get help from the big 6 then I wouldn't be good."

—Dan, second grade

"I learned how to use the big 6 proces better, to work with some and cowoporate with a boy as a partner, and to use the exiplepedia (encyclopedia) a little better."

—Josie, third grade

"(I learned) the 'Big 6', how to take notes, use information from the library, what a pamphlet would look like, to work well when your with a partner, to do my best work on everything. (Next time I will) include population, take my time, don't rush. It was fun to thing we were kind of like a state goverment."

—Arianne, third grade

As evidenced by the previous quotes, primary-age students are capable of self-evaluation when asked developmentally appropriate questions. Even non- and emerging readers can start to think about their success in the steps of the information search process as well as those affective questions that help them gain insight into interpersonal relationships.

Introducing Strategies for Big6 #6 How Will We Know If We Did Well?

Getting Started: Planning

Kindergartners and some beginning first graders may not yet have skills to perform a written evaluation. They can, however, answer questions orally as they work on or turn in their products. Ask questions such as, "Did I finish my work? Is my work neat? Did I work well with my group? What did I learn?" In addition, non-readers and writers can color in pictures that correspond to written answers such as a happy face for a positive response and a frowning face for one that is negative in value.

Consider giving students in first through third grades a set of directed, developmentally appropriate questions to which they will respond in writing. These questions should relate to students' perceptions about experiences with the information and in working with others. Having to articulate ideas in written form will ensure that the students think deeply and make connections that otherwise would be lost in the process. Teachers and library media specialists can easily determine the benefits and less desirable outcomes of the assignment and gather evidence of affective behaviors, such as attitudes towards learning and cooperative work, which would otherwise be difficult to assess. Require students to submit the written evaluation along with notes and final result as appropriate.

Students can answer questions such as: What did I learn? What skill did I learn that I can use again? How can I use it? What did I do well on my project? What could I do better next time? Did I include the information I found out about my subject? What did I contribute to my group? What did I like most about doing this project? (See Figure 9.4)

These guides are easily created using word processing software. Allow plenty of room for students to write and adequate time for completing the questions. Students in grades 2 and 3 can complete an online survey as the final evaluation of their project. The teachers or library media specialists can easily create one using Survey Monkey <http://www.surveymonkey.com> or another online survey creator.

Write the questions that you want students to answer in the self-evaluation portion of the process. Decide if students will answer the questions orally when they turn in their final product or if they will complete a written evaluation. If the evaluation is oral, write the questions on a large chart tablet or on the board. If it is written, make enough copies for the each child in the class.

Delivering Instruction

Sing the Big6 #6 verse (with the puppet if you are using one, see Chapter 10) and have students sing the refrain. Tell students that they will check their work and answer some questions about using the Big6 and about what they learned. Depending on its format—oral or written—give instructions for the evaluation. Students then complete the self-evaluation.

Big6 #6 How will I know if I did well?

Name: _____

1. What did I learn?

2. How well did I do on my _____?

Great! I did my   Pretty well. I almost   Not very well. I could   I did not try hard and
best work!   did my best work.   do better next time.   did not do my best.

3. Did I include the things I found out about my _____?

Yes! I included   I left out one   I did not include
everything!   or two facts.   the facts I found.

4. Did I work well with my Big6 Buddy?

Yes!   Most of the time   No

5. What did I do well this time?

6. What could I do better next time?

7. What did I like most about doing this project?

Created by Barbara A. Jansen, 1995.

Figure 9.2 Evaluating the Big6 Process

Evaluate Yourself Using the Big6™

By Barbara A. Jansen and Robert E. Berkowitz

Name: _____

Date: _____

Before you turn in your assignment or project, think about and
respond to the items below.

Big6 #1: What do I need to do?	■ Does the information in your final product answer the questions you wrote in Big6 #1? ■ Does your final product meet your teacher's expectations?
Big6 #2: What can I use to find what I need?	■ Did the books, Web sites, and other resources you used have the information you needed? ■ Did you select the best sources available to you? How do you know?
Big6 #3: Where can I find what I need?	■ Did you find the sources you needed? ■ Did you find the information you needed in each source?
Big6 #4: What information can I use?	■ Were you able to find information you needed? ■ Were you able to take notes or gather information?
Big6 #5: How can I show what I learned?	■ Did you organize your information? ■ Does your product present the information clearly?
Big6 #6: How will I know if I did well?	■ Did you do everything your teacher asked? ■ Did you use your time well?

Figure 9.3 Second and Third Grade Writing Evaluation

Checklist for a Writing Assignment Grades 2 and 3

By Barbara A. Jansen and Robert E. Berkowitz

Name: _____

Before you show your paper to others, make sure it is as perfect as possible. You should be proud to put your name on your paper.

You should be able to answer "yes" to all of these questions before you turn in your paper:

Did you do everything in the assignment and include all that was required for the paper?

____ yes   ____ no

Does your final paper show your original ideas as well as other information you found?

____ yes   ____ no

Did you give credit to all of your sources in a list (bibliography) at the end of your paper?

____ yes   ____ no

Did you use a word processor (or is your paper very neatly typed or hand-written if you do not have access to a computer)?

____ yes   ____ no

Is your paper complete and does it include a title page with heading information (title, your name, your teacher's name, date, etc.)

____ yes   ____ no

If your teacher asks for these, did you include your notes, copies of each version of your paper, and your list of books, people, and Web sites?

____ yes   ____ no

Would you be proud for anyone to read this paper?

____ yes   ____ no

Figure 9.4 Example of First Grade Evaluation

Name: _____ 1. $\underline{Da\ h\ a}$

$Dane$ 2. _____

1. What did I learn?

finding wreaking with Big
a Home six In
for To de the Libres

2. How well did I do on my _____?

Great! I did my best work!

Pretty well. I almost did my best work.

Not very well. I could do better next time.

I did not try hard and did not do my best.

3. Did I include the things I found out about my _____?

Yes! I included everything!

I left out one or two facts.

I did not include the facts I found.

Created by Barbara A. Jansen, 1995.

PART 3
Strategies for Implementation

The first two sections of this book set out the theoretical framework of the
Big6, and, in general terms, describe application strategies. This is certainly
valuable, but teachers also want to see how the Big6 works in real classroom
situations. That is the purpose of Part 3: to present the Big6 in the context of
content-area curricula, to encourage literature appreciation, and to learn
about specific components of the school library.

Individual, Small Group, and Whole Class Instruction

Depending on the topic and the developmental stage of your students, you
may choose to organize the instruction for individual learners, for small
groups, or by whole class. Most early learners will benefit from group work
at least for Big6 #1 through #4. Individually students can complete steps 5
and 6. However, completing all steps independently may prove difficult for

even the brightest second and third graders. They will need much attention and intervention throughout the process. Kindergartners and first graders should work with whole and small group assignments.

Whole class instruction works well when you want the class to find and use information 1) on a single topic, such as spiders, or 2) on one concept, such as "what life was like in 1492," especially if there is only one book that satisfies the need. Students are often sitting at the feet of the teacher who is reading aloud from a book or pointing to a computer monitor. The notes are taken from the source on a chart tablet or marker board for the whole class to use (see Chapter 7). This is often referred to as "carpet time." Or, students may be at tables or desks watching the overhead display as the teacher reads from the text or shows illustrations.

Configuring students in small groups for Big6 #3, Big6 #4, and Big6 #5 allows for a broader study of the topic—each group studies a particular animal (hyena, javelina, and rattlesnake) or community helper (firefighter, policeman, and teacher). Big6 #1 and Big6 #2 are completed in the whole group, then students work with Big6 Buddies (see next section) for *Location and Access* and *Use of Information*. *Synthesis* can be accomplished in the same small groups or individually, again depending on the developmental level of the students and on time factors. Often the Big6 Buddies will be employed to assist with the *Synthesis* step. The final step of the Big6, *Evaluation*, usually occurs on an individual basis (see Chapter 9).

Second and third grade students can begin working in small groups beginning with *Task Definition—What do we need to do?* They can brainstorm questions to answer with one or two partners. This configuration works well for each step of the Big6 when the class studies one topic, Native Americans for example, and each group assumes the responsibility of one subtopic, such as the Comanches or the Tonkawas.

Big6 Buddies

After whole group discussion to determine task and best sources, Big6 #3 and Big6 #4, and often Big6 #5, prove difficult for young learners to accomplish alone. Teachers, the library media specialist, instructional aides, and parents can certainly move among groups, monitoring progress and answering questions. Often, however, young learners may not know what questions to ask or even realize that they are in need of help, drifting away from the project at hand when the teacher is with another group. Using older helpers—"Big6 Buddies"—will assist young students in those steps that may exceed their capabilities while keeping them focused.

The Big6 Buddy helps the young researchers locate and use sources of information. They are assigned to one to two kindergartners, first graders, or second graders—"Little Buddies." The teacher may have already introduced the topic to her class, taking the students through Big6 #1 and Big6 #2 in whole group instruction. Big6 Buddies help with Big6 #3, Big6 #4, and sometimes Big6 #5 *Synthesis*. They assist the young learners in locating the needed source. Then they engage in the source in the appropriate manner. If the source is text, the Big6 Buddy will first direct the Little Buddies to the question in which they should listen for an answer. Then the Big6 Buddy will show how he accesses the appropriate section and begin reading the text that answers the question. The Little Buddies listen for the answers to the question, stopping the reader to identify the appropriate text.

The Big6 Buddy helps record the answer on the note taking organizer, then continues the process for the next questions. If the answers to questions can be taken from illustrations, the Big6 Buddy directs the Little Buddies to find "answers" in the photographs or illustrations, then helps record those words on the organizer. The young children should dictate to the Big6 Buddy, who will write verbatim on the organizer. If the Little Buddies are used to sharing the pen (see Chapter 3), the teacher can give the Big6 Buddies an abbreviated lesson on how to allow the children the opportunity of helping with their own note taking. With guidance, some first and most second graders can write their own notes.

It may be necessary to use more than one source of information. Locating and using one at a time gives groups access to needed sources and lessens confusion and distraction. Determine ahead of time specific Web sites and databases children will use and make bookmarks or links for easy access, or have Big6 Buddies manage information stations (see Chapter 6).

If the project requires the Big6 Buddies to help the Little Buddies with *Synthesis*, prepare the needed materials and instruct both parties in their responsibilities, reminding the Big6 Buddies to allow the Little Buddies to do most of the work. Having the Big6 Buddies assist in planning or sketching before the Little Buddy constructs the final product independently is an effective use of skills and an efficient use of time.

Adult helpers, of course, make your job much easier, as they require little direction and can control their Little Buddies with more authority. Any professional or paraprofessional can help. Send an email or note to the entire faculty and staff, asking for helpers, noting the time and date. Parent assistance works very well. Several days prior to the lesson, send home a note which reads something like the one sent by Brenda Lander, first grade teacher at Live Oak Elementary in Round Rock, Texas.

March 18, 2009

Dear Parents,

I'm sure by now you have heard all about Big6 and Big6 Buddies, but how would you like to have a chance to see the Big6 at work and actually be an active participant? On Tuesday, March 26, the children, Mrs. Dixon, Mrs. Jansen and I will be researching information about the desert as one of the biomes in our science curriculum. We have previously done research on the farm and on the cowboy using 5th grade Big6 Buddies. This time we would like to have parents be our Big6 Buddies and help your first graders find desert information in the library.

We will begin at 10:30 a.m. in the library. You can stay and have lunch with your child and we will complete our project after lunch by 1:00 p.m. If you are interested and would like to help us, please complete the bottom of this sheet and return it to me by Friday, March 22.

Once again, thank you for all you do. We couldn't do it without you.

Sincerely,
Brenda Lander

_____

I can help with the Big6 Research on Tuesday, March 26.

_____   _____
          Name   Phone number

____ I would like to order a lunch from the cafeteria. (Cost $4.00)

Fifth grade students and older make excellent Big6 Buddies for kindergartners, first graders, and second graders. The benefits to the older students include:

- Being put into a position of importance and responsibility
- Providing additional practice for Big6 #3 and Big6 #4 without engaging in the entire process in their curriculum
- Giving students who struggle academically a role in which they can succeed

Once the initial contact with the fifth grade (or other) teacher has taken place and the project scheduled, the library media specialist or teacher meets with the older students detailing their role as Big6 Buddies. She models how the Big6 Buddies will assist with Big6 #3 and Big6 #4 and to what extent they will help record notes (this is dependent, of course, on the age of the Little Buddies). If students will share the pen the teacher instructs the Big6 Buddies on the strategies they will use to promote conventional writing.

The primary teacher will make a list of the groups in order to facilitate the actual day. She also directs the Little Buddies in the expectations in their behavior with the Big6 Buddies. If any problems occur or discipline situations arise, the Big6 Buddy should inform a teacher immediately. Note: In the 10 years that I employed Big6 Buddies, the enthusiasm of the groups kept discipline problems to a minimum or they did not occur at all.

CHAPTER 10
Integrating the Big6 across the K-3 Curriculum

Guiding Questions

- How does the Big6 fit into state academic standards and tested skills?
- How can teachers and library media specialists further engage young learners in the process by using puppets, the Big6 song, and the Big6 poem?
- How does an integrated unit of study look for kindergarten, first, second, and third grades?

The Big6 and State Academic Standards for Grades K-3

Integrating the Big6 within subject-area content satisfies multiple state-mandated curriculum standards, including many that are tested annually on high stakes exams. Even though students are not usually tested until third grade, consider the objectives that may be covered when students are writing and using technology within the regular curriculum in language arts (reading and writing), math, social studies, science, health, or other subjects. Correlating the Big6 process and individual steps with your state's prescribed curriculum standards and skills tested on the state's annual performance exam proves that when students engage in the Big6 process they are doing so in a meaningful way. By the very nature of the process, students are interacting with content and skills standards and practicing those tested skills in a meaningful and authentic manner instead of merely completing practice worksheets. In the following figures you will find a correlation of the Big6 Skills and the Texas Assessment of Knowledge and Skills for English Language Arts tested at grade 3 (Figure 10.1) and a correlation of Big6 Skills and the Texas Essential Knowledge and Skills for a portion of English Language Arts for grade 2 (Figure 10.2).

Figure 10.1 Correlation of TAKS English Language Arts with Big6 Skills

Correlation between Big6 Skills and Texas Assessment of Knowledge & Skills

Big6™ Skills	TAKS English Language Arts Grade 3
4. Use of information— What information can we use?	(3.7) Reading/variety of texts. The student reads widely for different purposes in varied sources. The student is expected to (B) read from a variety of genres to aquire information [from both print and electronic sources].
4. Use of Information— What information can we use? **5. Synthesis—How can we put our information together?**	(3.9) Reading/comprehension. The student uses a variety of strategies to comprehend selections read aloud and selections read independently. The student is expected to (F) make and explain inferences from texts such as determining important ideas, causes and effects, making predictions, and drawing conclusions; (H) produce summaries of text selections; (I) represent text information in different ways, including story maps, graphs, and charts; and (J) distinguish fact from opinion in various texts, including news stories and advertisements.
4. Use of Information— What information can we use?	(3.11) Reading/text structures/literary concepts. The student analyzes the characteristics of various types of texts. The student is expected to (C) recognize the distinguishing features of familiar genres, including stories and informational texts.

Figure 10.2 Correlation of TEKS English Language Arts with Big6 Skills

Correlation between Big6 Skills and Texas Essential Knowledge & Skills for English Language Arts (Texas curriculum standards for Grade 2)

Big6™ Skills	TEKS English Language Arts (partial) Grade 2
1.1 Define the problem **1.2 Identify the information needed**	2.12 (A) Identify relevant questions for inquiry such as "What Native American tribes inhabit(ed) Texas?"
3.1 Locate sources **3.2 Access information within source**	2.12 (B) Use alphabetical order to locate information; (C) recognize and use parts of a book to locate information, including table of contents, chapter titles, guide words, and indices
4.1 Engage in sources **4.2 Extract relevant information**	2.12 (D) Use multiple sources, including print such as an encyclopedia, technology, and experts, to locate information that addresses questions
4.1 Engage in sources **4.2 Extract relevant information**	2.12 (E) Interpret and use graphic sources of information including maps, charts, graphs, and diagrams
3.1 Locate sources **3.2 Access information within source**	2.12 (F) Locate and use important areas of the library media center
5.1 Organize information from a variety of sources **5.2 Present results**	2.12 (G) Demonstrate learning through productions and displays such as oral and written reports, murals, and dramatizations; (H) draw conclusions from information gathered.
5.1 Organize information from a variety of sources **5.2 Present results**	2.14 (A) Write to record ideas and reflections; (B) write to discover, develop, and refine ideas; (C) write to communicate with a variety of audiences; (D) write in different forms for different purposes

The blank correlation documents (Figures 10.3, 10.4, and 10.5) will help you get started on making your own correlation. Library media specialists will want to complete these for all grades and subjects, helping them justify to teachers and administrators the importance of integrated information and communications technology skills within the framework of the Big6. The correlations prove that Big6 is not an "add-on" to the curriculum, but an integral part of it, which is included in the state's exams and curriculum standards. Create blank word-processing tables for other subject areas such as math, foreign language, health, career options, physical education, and fine arts, or use the templates included on the accompanying CD-ROM.

Figure 10.3 Blank Correlation for Big6 and Social Studies Standards

Correlation between Big6 Skills
and State Curriculum Standards or Tested Skills

Big6™ Skills	Social Studies Objectives Grade(s):
The entire Big6 process can be used to support the mastery of all history; government, geography; economics; culture; science, technology, and society; and citizenship content objectives in social studies.	**All content objectives:** history; government; geography; economics; culture; science, technology, and society; and citizenship
Big6 Skill(s)	Curriculum standard or tested skills:
Big6 Skill(s)	Curriculum standard or tested skills:
Big6 Skill(s)	Curriculum standard or tested skills:
Big6 Skill(s)	Curriculum standard or tested skills:
Big6 Skill(s)	Curriculum standard or tested skills:

Correlation between Big6 Skills
and State Curriculum Standards or Tested Skills

Big6™ Skills	English Language Arts Objectives Grade(s):
Big6 Skill(s)	Curriculum standard or tested skills:
Big6 Skill(s)	Curriculum standard or tested skills:
Big6 Skill(s)	Curriculum standard or tested skills:
Big6 Skill(s)	Curriculum standard or tested skills:
Big6 Skill(s)	Curriculum standard or tested skills:
Big6 Skill(s)	Curriculum standard or tested skills:

Figure 10.5 Blank Correlation for Big6 and Science Standards

Correlation between Big6 Skills
and State Curriculum Standards or Tested Skills

Big6™ Skills	Science Objectives Grade(s):
The entire Big6 process can be used to support the mastery of all content objectives in science such as weather, animal adaptation, rocks and minerals, habitats, planets, light, sound, and the senses.	**All content objectives:** general, life, and earth science; including human body systems, solar system, water cycle
Big6 Skill(s)	Curriculum standard or tested skills:
Big6 Skill(s)	Curriculum standard or tested skills:
Big6 Skill(s)	Curriculum standard or tested skills:
Big6 Skill(s)	Curriculum standard or tested skills:
Big6 Skill(s)	Curriculum standard or tested skills:

Using Puppets, the Big6 Song, and the Big6 Poem to Engage Young Learners

Remember the first grade class in Chapter 1 that could not take its collective eyes off Celestine the Toad puppet as she took them through the steps of the Big6? She sang to them and told her Big6 story, keeping their attention for sessions longer than usual. Second graders listened as Maybelle the cow puppet questioned "why any self-respecting cow would want to jump over the moon when she has such a nice home on earth," leading students into a study of the solar system. Kindergartners enjoyed Clarice, the opera singing tarantula puppet, as she helped them learn about spiders and why they are beneficial to people.

No matter the quality of the performance by the teacher or library media specialist, it is the author's opinion that the non-judgmental children will think your effort is wonderful. They hardly even pay any attention to the person controlling the puppet. You do not need a professional-quality voice; simply changing voices for each puppet raises students' interest that much higher. The children think it is hilarious when each puppet has a unique personality and talks and sings in its own voice—the sillier the better.

Getting Started with Puppets

Use any puppet—it will work. However, animal puppets that have a realistic-looking appearance lend an air of authenticity to the topic. I found that the Folkmanis line of animal puppets <http://folkmanis.com> worked nicely with my young students. Most have workable mouths that allow you to insert your full hand (see Figure 10.6), making it easier to manipulate the puppet and giving it the appearance of spoken word. As the Folkmanis or any puppets can be costly, you may need to build your collection over time. Consider purchasing puppets for each classification of animal in which your primary students study including mammals, amphibians, birds, fish, reptiles, insects, and spiders.

Practice hand movements in front of a mirror without using a puppet. Talk about anything as you move your hand in sync with your mouth. With your fingers stiff, your thumb close to your fingers (your hand shaped similar to a crocodile's mouth—see Figure 10.7) open and close your hand in time to your words, not quite touching your fingers to your thumb. When you finish a talking or take a pause, close your hand so that your fingers are resting on your thumb; as in real life, one's mouth closes completely when finished talking. Once your hand is in sync with your spoken words, practice with the

Tip: *Visit the Axtell Expressions Web site for more tips on puppeteering and puppet manipulation available <http://axtell.com/manip.html>.*

Figure 10.6 Puppet with Large, Workable Mouth

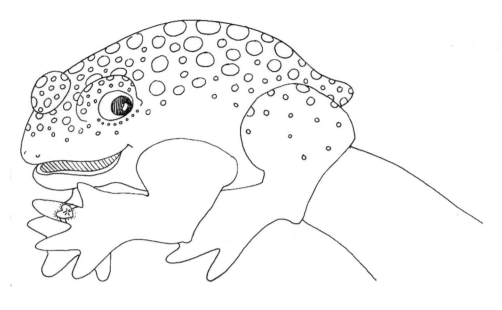

Figure 10.7 Correct Position for Hand in Puppet's Mouth

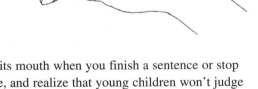

puppet, making sure to close its mouth when you finish a sentence or stop talking. Don't be shy, practice, and realize that young children won't judge you. After several attempts in front of a class, your inhibitions will disappear as you notice the zeal with which your students respond.

Try to connect the type of puppet with the content of the topic. For example, use a wolf when studying the characteristics of mammals. Obvious connections are using a bat or spider when studying those specific species. If you have one animal for each classification of vertebrates, including some invertebrates (spiders and insects), you can also use those puppets to tie into other areas of the curriculum.

Additional Uses of Puppets in the Curriculum:

- **Farm life**: A cow or dog.

- **Solar system**: A cow (see the first paragraph in this section).

- **Forest biome**: A spider or other woodland creature.

- **The sea or ocean**: Fish puppet.

- **Pond life**: Frog, dragonfly, or fish puppet.

- **Healthy habits**: Have any puppet talk about not feeling good and pretend to take its temperature using a thermometer or put your hand on its "forehead."

- **Time or daily schedule**: Put a watch on the arm of a puppet.

- **United States symbols**: Stick an American flag pin on any puppet to begin a conversation.

- **Community helpers or careers**: Put a stethoscope around a puppet's neck or a little fire hat on one's head.

- **Map skills**: Have a puppet try unsuccessfully to use a globe or map.

- **Seasons**: Put a little scarf around a puppet's neck or a pair of sunglasses on its head.

- **Transportation**: Use a fish or bird puppet to begin talking about how animals and people get around.

- **Community government**: Pin a "Vote for me" button on a puppet.

- **Weather or water cycle**: Hold an umbrella over you and the puppet.

- **Living and nonliving**: Have your puppet bump into a child and say "excuse me" or "pardon me." Have the puppet comment or notice when the child reacts. Then have the puppet bump into a chair and say "excuse me" or "pardon me." When the chair does not respond in any way, have the puppet question why.

- **Needs of living things**: Have a conversation with any animal puppet about what they need to live (you can make this humorous for the children by arguing with the puppet when it says it needs a sports car or flat-screen TV).

- **Rocks and soil**: Have any puppet talk about an interesting rock it found on the way to school.

You get the idea! Use your imagination and watch the children's excitement grow whenever they see a puppet appear on your hand.

More puppet tips

Use one puppet per topic since more than one becomes difficult to manage. If you have several puppets that you use throughout the year, develop unique personalities and voices for each. This keeps the students' interest level high and helps them make connections with each puppet. No matter the unit, they will remember each puppet's name and unique characteristics. Children look forward to learning from:

- Clarice, the opera-singing tarantula, who performed at the Metropolitan Opera in New York City before coming back to her native Arizona. She has a high-pitched cultured voice and a somewhat superior, but kind attitude. She teaches the children to sing the Big6 song in an operatic voice with trilling Rs.

- Celestine, the toad with has a sweet southern drawl and a slow wit about her. She is convinced the diamond rings on her "fingers" were given to her by the Queen of England from the royal jewel collection.

- Charles, the rattlesnake who speaks with a lisp and shrewdly teaches the students about the four poisonous snakes in the United States.

- Vincent, the bat whose high-pitched thin voice and timid nature make it difficult for him to speak in public. Children help him overcome his shyness.

- Alexander, the wolf who has a big goofy voice and personality.

- Maybelle, the cow whose voice sounds quite "country," who loves to check out good library books to read aloud to her farm friends.

Using the Big6 Song and the Big6 Poem

Accompanying the steps of the Big6 with a song or poem also engages the interest of the students and adds a level of repetition to the effort. When their teacher, library media specialist, or puppet friend sings to them, children will pay close attention and make additional connections to the steps of the Big6. Sing a verse of the Big6 Song as you introduce each step. If you are using a puppet, it can do the singing and help the children learn the song. The class may only remember the refrain and should be encouraged to sing it each time. See the Big6 Song and the Big6 Poem on the following pages.

The Big6 Song

(Sung to the tune of "B-I-N-G-O")
Words by Barbara A. Jansen, 1994.

There is a process I can use and Big6 is its name-o

Refrain:

B-I-G S-I-X, B-I-G S-I-X, B-I-G S-I-X,
and Big6 is its name-o.

Big6 One will help me find out just what I should do-O.

(Refrain)

Big6 Two will help me choose those things that I
should use-O.

(Refrain)

Big6 Three will help me get those things that I will need-O.

(Refrain)

Big6 Four helps me to take out words that I can use-O.

(Refrain)

Big6 Five helps me finish the work that I must do-O.

(Refrain)

Big6 Six helps me to know if I did my best work-O.

(Refrain)

The Big6 Poem

Use the Big6 Poem with second and third graders. You or the puppet can recite each verse upon introducing that step in the process. Consider varying the traditional cadence with a rap beat. As you introduce each step of the Big6 in the context of the curriculum, recite the accompanying verse and ask students if they can explain what it means. Discuss the meaning of each step before you give details for that particular assignment.

Written by Barbara A. Jansen, 1994.

When I have something that needs to be done,
And I need information because I have none,
I'll use my tools that help me do
The job that I'm happy to share with you.
The Big6 will help me find what I need,
And put it together, I can do it, indeed!

When I have a task, that is something to do,
And I need information to do it because it is new.
Big6 #1 will help me succeed
By figuring out just what exactly I need.

Big6 #2 will help me choose
When I decide just what I can use.
I'll choose the ones that meet my needs best,
I may choose two or three and leave all the rest.

Where, oh where, can I find these things now?
In a book? On the Web? And **Big6 #3** tells me how
To find those people or print that I chose,
And get to where my information is located in those.

Read, look, and listen is what I'll do when
I use **Big6 #4** to get just what I need and then
I'll write it or draw the information I find.
I'll get what I need because I'll use my mind.

Once I have found and written all that I need,
I must put it together so I can proceed
To finish the job and show it, you see.
And **Big6 #5** will surely help me.

How will I know if I did my job well?
Big6 #6 will sure help me to tell
If I did it the best that I possibly could,
And do it better next time if I should.

Integrating the Big6 in Content Areas: Lesson Plans

In the lesson plans that follow, specific curriculum standards are not included due to the variations in wording from state to state. Of course, teachers should use these plans as guides for designing instruction, making modifications to meet the requirements of their subject-area, state-prescribed curriculum and the developmental levels of their students. They should include the specific standards of their state or district. While the titles of the lessons may sound like one subject area—social studies, science, etc.—take a look at the content objectives because multiple subjects are integrated into each plan, in addition to information and communications technology skills. The plans indicate a grade level only as a guide for the developmental appropriateness of the activities, not necessarily for the content covered, as curriculum varies across grades from state to state.

The time estimate is just that—an estimate. The time will vary for a particular class's level of experience with each step of the Big6 and the skills within the steps, and for modifications made in the plan. In addition, some elements of a lesson may be written into a plan, such as a scoring rubric, but may not actually be included. Of course, teachers who modify these plans for their state or district's curriculum will create the missing pieces to complete the plan for their students.

When recording the task and questions to be answered, consider sharing the pen—interactive writing—with your students (for more information, see Chapter 3). While not specifically stated in each lesson plan, this practice fits nicely in all lessons and allows for interaction among students in the class and a greater understanding of the task. In addition, students gain numerous benefits from sharing the pen in various settings.

These lessons are for demonstration purposes only. You will want to take ideas from them, explore other approaches and possibilities, and adapt the content to your program's and students' needs and available technology. Consideration must be taken into account and accommodations made for students who have learning or language challenges (see section about differentiating instruction in Chapter 3). Notice, also, that while the six steps of the process include the sub-skills, they are not labeled for kindergarten through third grade—the main six steps are all they need. Third grade teachers can certainly begin to use the original language of the Big6 along with the sub-skills—the Little 12—with their classes.

Each lesson provides for collaboration among the classroom teacher, library media specialist, and technology teacher (if applicable). Other teachers, such as art and music, may also collaborate with the classroom teachers to bring further expertise into the mix. In the examples, "teacher" refers to the adult leading that portion of the lesson. See collaboration strategies in Chapter 3 for ideas on responsibilities of the teacher and library media specialist in lesson planning and instructional delivery.

Lesson Plan Going Batty

Grade: Kindergarten

Content objectives: Ask questions about organisms; identify basic needs of organisms; recognize dependence of living organisms on one another

Information skills objectives: Listen and respond to sources of information; follow oral directions; determine purpose for listening; listen to texts read aloud; use pictures and print to gather information and answer questions; write to record ideas

Time estimate: Three or four 30-minute sessions

Information problem and overarching question: Vincent the bat puppet greets students and begins a conversation about finding a little bat on the ground and not knowing what to do with it. He knows that bats must be important and wants to save the little one. (If you cannot find a bat puppet, show a simple picture of a bat and have another puppet—or yourself—begin the conversation.) The teacher suggests that Vincent use the Big6 to help find out about bats so he can make a decision on what to do with the little bat. (If students are not familiar with the Big6, the teacher tells Vincent, "It is a set of steps we can use when we need to find out something because we have a job to do or something to figure out, such as what to do with the little bat on the ground." Children should be taught to avoid bats on the ground as they are vectors for rabies.) Vincent introduces the Big6 by singing the first verse of the Big6 Song. Write below step 1, "Learn about bats. How are bats important to the animal and human world?"

Big6 #1: What do we need to do?

1. Vincent sings the Big6 #1 verse and shows students the poster of the Big6 (see Appendix A.) Together, he reads as he points to each word *What do we need to do?* and asks children to read with him as he reads and points again. Vincent sings the verse for Big6 #1 and helps the class with the refrain, asking them to sing along with him. Ask the class, "What does Vincent need to do?," listening and responding to students' answers. Eventually, tell students, "We need to learn about bats to see if we can figure out what to do with a bat found on the ground." (Depending on the area of the United States in which the class resides, you may need to change the problem somewhat if no bats live in your area. Consider using a zookeeper who discovers a live baby bat on the ground in the bat enclosure.)

2. The teacher now asks the class what they would like to learn about bats and helps them record those questions on chart paper. She adds some questions of her own if the children don't think of them: Are bats harmful to humans? Why shouldn't we touch bats we find on the ground? How is a bat similar to

a dog? How is it similar to a bird? How do bats help our world? How do bats move? When are bats active? Do bats carry diseases? What should Vincent do with the little bat? How are bats important to the animal and human world?

3. If a student asks if bats eat bugs, she says, "Let's write, 'What do bats eat?,' instead." If another student wants to know if bats eat mice, she can ask the class which question will help them get the answer. Then, she points to and reads, "What do bats eat?," and has the class read along while she point to each word.

Big6 #2: What can we use to find what we need?

Vincent sings the verse for Big6 #2, asking students to sing the refrain. The teacher (ideally this person is the library media specialist) discusses with the class and Vincent the best ways to find the answers to the questions. They decide that books and Web sites will be the best ways to find the answers. A local zoo is a good source also. The teacher records the sources on the Big6 chart.

Big6 #3: Where can we find what we need?

Vincent sings the verse for Big6 #3, asking students to sing the refrain. The teacher (ideally this is the library media specialist) reads the question *Where can we find what we need?* to the class and points to each word as she reads it. She talks to the class about finding the sources, books and Web sites, or making a call to the zoo to speak to someone about the bats. Show students the section of the library where they would find bat books. Tell them how you found a good Web site about bats and why it is a good site.

Big6 #4: What information can we use?

Discuss with the children how Big6 #4 helps us find answers to our questions. Vincent sings the verse for Big6 #4 and the children sing the refrain. The teacher reads the question *What information can we use?* to the class and points to each word as she reads it. Begin the note taking triad strategy (see Chapter 8) with one adult reading the book or Web site and the other adult recording answers to questions as identified by students. Focus on only one question at a time. Share the pen as appropriate. When the answer is found about how bats move, have students pretend to be a bat and move around the room with their arms extended and fingers spread out like those in a bat's wings. Continue until all questions are answered. Include on the chart tablet the name of the book and Web site used. Tell students that we give credit (or "thanks") to the sources that help us answer our questions.

Big6 #5: How can we put our information together?

1. Tell students now that they have answered their questions, Big6 #5 will help put the answers together into some form they can use. Vincent sings the verse to Big6 #5 and the children sing the refrain. The teacher reads

the question *How can we put our information together?* to the class and points to each word as she reads it. Tell students that they will make a book about bats.

2. Demonstrate the assembly of the book. The body and pages should be precut. Tell students that the first page of their book will contain one fact that they like about bats with a drawing of it. The second page will answer the question, "What should Vincent do with the baby bat he found on the ground?" The third page should answer the question, "How are bats useful to us?" Their teacher or library media specialist (or other adult helper) will help them write those "answers" or draw pictures.

3. One wing should have their name and the other wing should have the name of the book and Web site copied from the note chart. They should ask an adult to help if needed.

4. The teacher should show students a completed book before they start.

5. Depending on the time of year and the developmental level of students in the class, directions for the completion of the book may need to be given and followed one at a time.

Big6 #6: How will we know if we did well?

When students are finished with their books, talk about Big6 #6 and have Vincent sing that verse with the children joining in the refrain. The teacher reads the question *How will we know if we did well?* to the class and points to each word as she reads it. Then have the class read the question. Ask the students to individually answer these questions: Did you do the very best that you could? How do you know? Repeat the questions, this time having children answer orally. Have children exchange books with a partner for evaluation. The partner tells what he or she likes about the book.

Assessment:

Each child should be able to articulate how bats are helpful and how a grounded baby bat should be treated. Each child should successfully follow oral directions.

Lesson Plan   Old MacDonald's Farm

Grade: First

Content objectives: Identify examples of and describe how people in the community use natural resources; describe how certain jobs contribute to the production of goods and services; create simple maps using the four cardinal directions; group living organisms and nonliving objects; identify basic needs; distinguish fiction from nonfiction; participate in songs and discussions

Information skills objectives: Determine purpose for listening; ask and answer relevant questions; use pictures, print, and people to gather information and answer questions; write to record ideas; record or dictate own knowledge of a topic

Technology skills objectives: Use technology to compose text and illustrations

Time estimate: Four or five 30 to 45-minute sessions

Information problem and overarching question: Maybelle the cow is moving from the library to Old MacDonald's farm which better suits her needs, as there is no grass for grazing nor a good place to sleep in the library. She doesn't know what to expect in the way of living arrangements, her new animal and people friends, or getting to know the farm as well as she does the library. What can Maybelle expect from the farm? Why is the farm important to Maybelle and the community?

Big6 #1: What do we need to do?

1. Introduce the information problem to the class by having a conversation with Maybelle the cow puppet (change the animal if needed). How can we help Maybelle learn about her new home? Discuss possibilities with the class, then summarize by saying, "What we need to do is help Maybelle learn all about life on the farm and why farms are important." Maybelle gets visibly excited as she leads the class in the introduction and first verse of the Big6 Song, including the refrain. Point to Big6 #1 on the chart, read with the class *What do we need to do?*, and answer "Help Maybelle learn all about life on the farm and why it is an important place to the community."

2. Ask students what animals they think live on a farm and work together to create a list. Include only domesticated animals (cow, horse, chicken, donkey, dog, cat, pig, sheep, geese, etc.), not wild animals such as a rat or crow. Discuss the difference in domesticated and wild animals and the reason for only including domesticated animals.

3. Read a short picture book about a farm (such as *The Cow That Went OINK* by Bernard Most, Red Wagon Books, 1990), asking students to identify the animals and compare those to their list. Add any as needed. Ask students if they believe the animals in the book could actually live on a farm. What about the book makes it fiction (make believe) instead of factual (real)?

4. Sing "Old MacDonald Had a Farm" with the class, using the animals listed. (See end of the lesson for words. The National Institute of Environmental Health Sciences maintains a Web site for children that includes the words and sing-along music to "Old MacDonald" <http://kids.niehs.nih.gov/lyrics/mcdonald.htm>). Before singing, hand out a picture of a farm animal to each child in the class. There should be at least two to three children who have the same picture. When their animal's verse is sung, they should come to the front with the others in their group. This will form the groups for the project.

5. Tell the children that they should learn about the farm and how their animal helps the farmer. Ask the class what information they will need to find out. List their questions, modifying as needed, including:

   a. How does Old MacDonald use the natural resources on his land?

   b. How is my animal useful to Old MacDonald in providing goods for his family and to the community?

   c. What does my animal eat and drink?

   d. Where on the farm does my animal live?

   e. What is each member of my animal family called (father, mother, baby)?

   f. How many babies does it have?

6. Present brief lessons on natural resources and goods and services if the students have not previously studied these concepts.

Big6 #2: What can we use to find what we need?

Ask students if they know which step is next and have someone read it. Maybelle sings verse 2 and the refrain of the Big6 Song, encouraging the children to sing along. Discuss this step of the process, leading students to brainstorm ideas about how they can get answers to their questions. Write their ideas and add those sources that students omit. Tell students that books and Web sites will give the best answers for their questions. Of course, if the school is near or in a farming community, human resources and field trips will enrich the experience.

Big6 #3: Where can we find what we need?

Again, ask students, "Who knows which step is next?," and have someone read it. Maybelle sings verse 3 and the refrain of the Big6 Song, encouraging the children to sing along. Demonstrate the use of the library's catalog to show how to find informational books on farms and specific animals and tell the children that these books have been put on a special cart for the first graders to use. Show the Web sites students will use and tell why they are useful. Tell students that Big6 Buddies will be coming in to help them with the next step (see introduction to Part 3 for information on using Big6 Buddies).

Big6 #4: What information can we use?

1. (Bring in Big6 Buddies—fifth graders or parents—pairing one or two with each group of first graders, or choose another advantageous grouping of students. Instruct the fifth graders or parents ahead of time in ways they can help the Little Buddies and to what extent they should or shouldn't write the notes—answers to the questions—for them.)

2. Ask the first graders if someone can tell their Big6 Buddies on which step of the Big6 they will help with first (see the introduction to Part 3). Have a first grader point to the step on the Big6 chart for everyone to read. Maybelle sings verse 4 and the refrain of the Big6 Song, encouraging all of the children to sing along.

3. Hand out prepared data charts to each first grader (see Figure 10.8), telling them that their Big6 Buddies will help them record answers to their questions. Reinforce responsibilities of Big6 Buddies and Little Buddies before allowing the groups to work together to answer questions.

4. When all groups have finished taking notes, have the Little Buddies thank their Big6 Buddies before leaving.

Big6 5: How can we put our information together?

1. Ask students which step of the Big6 comes next. Have one point to the chart and read aloud with the class. Maybelle sings verse 5 and the refrain of the Big6 Song, as the children sing along.

2. Tell students that the class will create a slide show for Maybelle, using KidPix software (The Learning Company), that teaches her about the importance of the farm and the animals she can expect to meet.

3. Discuss with the class how Old MacDonald uses the natural resources for his farm (food produced by farming the land, a pond for the animal's drinking water, water from a faucet for the animals living in the barn, etc.). Draw a map on a slide, using a bird's-eye view that illustrates the farm, including a field of corn, the house, a fenced pasture, a pigpen, the barn, a pond, etc. Use text tools and voice recordings as appropriate. Label the map with the cardinal directions: north, south, east, and west. Or, if a KidPix slide seems too small, draw the map on large butcher paper.

Figure 10.8 Data Chart for Farm Animal Note Taking

Data Chart for Farm Animal Note Taking

Your names: Name of farm animal:	How is my animal useful to Old MacDonald in providing goods?	What does my animal eat and drink?	Where on the farm does my animal live?	What is each family member called (mother, father, baby)?	How many babies does it have?
Source 1 (Title author)					
Source 2 (Title, author)					
Source 3 (Title, author)					
Big6 Buddy (ies):					

5. Instruct each group to sketch on drawing paper a picture of their animal in its environment on the farm. The picture will include drawings of the animal and the appropriate number of babies, its food, and the area it lives on the farm (barn, corral, pasture, etc). On the sketch, the group should write how its animal is useful to Old MacDonald in providing goods for his family and to the community and what each family member is called. Their sketch should include plants and nonliving objects to make the scene look realistic. List these items for the class to reference while working. As the groups work on their sketches, the teachers should visit with each group to ensure that all components are included on the sketch.

6. Each group will create a slide from its sketch. Using the KidPix voice recorder, each child will record one prepared sentence (how the animal helps the farmer or what the animal's family members are called).

7. As a class, create an opening slide for Maybelle's show or ask the Big6 Buddy class to make one. Assemble the slides into a slide show, adding transitions and sounds. Present the slide show to Maybelle.

8. Looking at the map of the farm, have individual children give Maybelle oral directions to help her get around the farm. Examples: Your barn is east of the pond. Your pasture is west of the corn field. The pig's pen is north of Old MacDonald's house. Children can turn it into riddles for Maybelle: What is east of the pond? What is west of the corn field? An additional activity pairs students and has them take turns being Maybelle and giving her directions.

Big6 #6: How will we know if we did well?
Direct the students' attention to the Big6 chart. Ask students on which step they have not yet worked. Point to Big6 #6 and read it with the students. Maybelle sings verse 6 of the Big6 Song with students singing along.

Tell students that Big6 #6 *How will I know if I did well?* helps them figure out what they know and what they still need to learn. Each student will complete the self-evaluation (see Figure 10.9).

Assessment:
Create scoring guide including these items:
Group sketch and KidPix slide include:
- a picture of the animal in its environment on the farm
- drawings of the animal and the appropriate number of babies
- its food
- the area in which it lives on the farm
- words describing how the animal is useful to Old MacDonald in providing goods for his family and to the community
- the names of the mother, father, and baby
- nonliving objects to make the scene look realistic

Figure 10.9 Self-Evaluation for Farm Unit

Big6 #6 How will I know if I did well?

Name: _____

1. What did I learn?

2. How well did I do on my farm picture?

Great! I did my best work!   *Pretty well. I almost did my best work.*   *Not very well. I could do better next time.*   *I did not try hard and did not do my best.*

3. Did I include the things I found out about my animal?

Yes! I included everything!   *I left out one or two facts.*   *I did not include the facts I found.*

4. Did I work well with my partner?

Yes!   *Most of the time*   *No*

5. Did I work well with my Big6 Buddy?

Yes!   *Most of the time*   *No*

6. What did I do well this time?

7. What could I do better next time?

8. What did I like the most about doing this farm project?

©*Barbara A. Jansen, 1995, 2007.*

Individual responses include:

- one oral direction correctly using north, south, east, or west for Maybelle
- participation in class discussion and singing
- appropriate interaction with Big6 Buddy
- attempt at filling in data chart—most squares filled in correctly with help
- appropriate interaction with partners

Lesson extension: Read about or discuss and show pictures of corporate farming such as Archer Daniels Midland (<http://admworld.com/naen/>) and compare and contrast them to Old MacDonald's family farm.

Old MacDonald had a farm, E-I-E-I-O
And on his farm he had a cow, E-I-E-I-O
With a moo-moo here and a moo-moo there, here a moo, there a moo, every where a moo-moo,
Old MacDonald had a farm, E-I-E-I-O

Old MacDonald had a farm, E-I-E-I-O
And on his farm he had a pig, E-I-E-I-O
With an oink-oink here and an oink-oink there, here an oink, there an oink, every where an oink-oink,
Old MacDonald had a farm, E-I-E-I-O

Old MacDonald had a farm, E-I-E-I-O
And on his farm he had a horse, E-I-E-I-O
With a neigh-neigh here and a neigh-neigh there, here a neigh, there a neigh, every where a neigh-neigh,
Old MacDonald had a farm, E-I-E-I-O

Repeat verse for each animal on the class's list.

Lesson Plan   Life in Columbus's Day

> **Grade:** Second
>
> **Content objectives:** Identify how the community has changed over time; compare and contrast life today and long ago; explain how science and technology have changed how we fulfill basic needs; use vocabulary related to past, present, and future
>
> **Information skills objectives:** Identify relevant questions for inquiry; recognize and use parts of a book; represent, compare, and interpret data using tables, charts, and graphs; use knowledge of the author's purpose to understand informational text; use table of contents to locate information in text; ask and respond to questions; report on a topic with supporting facts and details; produce summaries of text selections; determine important ideas from text; recognize distinguishing features of informational texts
>
> **Technology skills objectives:** Use computer to publish results; demonstrate understanding of informational text in a variety of ways using available technology; use computerized drawing tools
>
> **Time estimate:** Three to five class periods
>
> **Information problem and overarching question:** How does a community change over time?

Big6 #1: What do we need to do?

1. In preparation for Columbus Day, read a short biography of Christopher Columbus. Ask students to each write on a piece of paper the reason he is important enough to have a holiday named after him. Ask for volunteers to read aloud their responses. On the board or chart paper, write the current year. Under it, write 1492 and have students help you subtract it from the current year:

$$\begin{array}{r} 2009 \\ -1492 \\ \hline 517 \end{array}$$

2. Start a conversation about what it would have been like to live 517 years ago. Present the introduction to the Big6 Poem and have the class read aloud in unison. Tell students that they will use the Big6 to help them find out about life in Columbus's time and compare and contrast it to their own.

3. Ask the class to read the verse containing Big6 #1 and have someone try to explain the meaning of the verse. Or, sing verse #1 of the Big6 Song. What do you want to know about life in 1492? As students give their suggestions, instead of writing "Did they have bicycles?" write "transportation." Continue

until the list reads: food, occupations, education, recreation, and transportation. Add categories as appropriate.

4. Divide the class into five groups or group them according to the number of categories on the list. If there are more than three or four students in any one group, reduce the size of the groups and assign the same topic to two or more groups.

5. Have each group brainstorm four questions that it is interested in learning about its topic. Monitor each group, helping students refine questions.

6. Demonstrate how to construct the note taking boxes sheet (see Chapter 7). Each student in the group folds the paper and writes one question at the top of each box.

Big6 #2: What can we use to find what we need?

Have the class read the verse containing Big6 #2 and ask someone to try to explain the meaning of the verse. Brainstorm with the class a list of sources each group can use to find answers to its questions. Narrow the list to the best available sources.

Big6 #3: Where can we find what we need?

1. Have the class read the verse containing Big6 #3 and ask someone to try to explain the meaning of the verse.

2. Demonstrate the library's online catalog to find a book on life in Columbus's time. (Consider Barbara Brenner, *If You Were There in 1492*, Bradbury Press, 1991.)

3. Using the social studies textbook, present a brief lesson on how to use the table of contents (see Chapter 6).

4. Search a children's subscription database (such as EBSCO's *Searchasaurus*), a subject directory (such as subscription-based *netTrekker* <http://nettrekker.com> or free Web site *KidsClick* <http://kidsclick.org>), and an online and on-shelf encyclopedia for appropriate materials.

5. Tell students that adult Big6 Buddies will be coming in to assist each group as it works through the various information stations (see Chapter 6): library book; on-shelf encyclopedia; and several computers, each designated for a specific sources, including online encyclopedia and several pre-selected Web sites or subject databases.

Big6 #4: What information can we use?

1. Have the class read the verse containing Big6 #4 and ask someone to try to explain the meaning of the verse.

2. Instruct each group to begin at one of the information stations. (Helpers have been instructed in how to connect children with the sources and the extent of

help the students may need.) The teacher or library media specialist should remain available if possible to assist groups as needed and to keep the groups moving through the stations. Groups should switch information stations every 15 or 20 minutes. This process may take two class periods.

3. Students rotate through each information station, recording appropriate answers in the note taking boxes. They must record source titles on the back of their organizer before they leave each station.

Big6 #5: How can we put our information together?

1. Have the class read the verse containing Big6 #5 and ask someone to try to explain the meaning of the verse.

2. In the computer lab, instruct students in using word processing drawing tools to create a Venn diagram (see Figure 10.10). Each group should use its notes to label and fill in the appropriate information.

Figure 10.10 Venn Diagram of Life in 1492 and Now

Life in 1492 and Now: Education

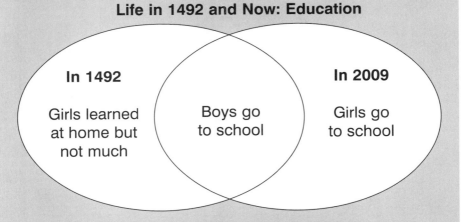

In 1492

Girls learned at home but not much

Boys go to school

In 2009

Girls go to school

3. Each group prints several copies of its diagram. Post the diagrams in several places in the classroom for easy access.

4. Each student will use the information from each diagram to write a story about a child who, on Columbus Day, wakes up in the year 1492 and tries to find a way back to present day. In the story, children need to include comparisons of life then and now. Students should follow steps of the writing process (see Appendix F for the Big6 Writing Process Organizer).

Big6 #6: How will we know if we did well?

The class reads the verse containing Big6 #6. Ask someone to explain the meaning of the verse. Individually, students compare their published written product to a checklist before turning it in. Additionally, each student completes an information evaluation of his or her experience with the Big6 process, including responding to questions such as: What information did I learn? What skills did I learn that I can use again? In what ways can I use the Big6 again? How did I contribute to my group? What did I do well? What could I do better next time? What did I like about this project?

Assessment:
Teachers can assess individuals' level of involvement in their groups and create and use a rubric for the written product (see Figure 10.11). Care should be taken in assessment for mastery of skills, as some skills may be beyond the developmental level of some second graders (see Chapter 2).

Figure 10.11 Sample Writing Rubric for Second Grade

Second Grade Writing Rubric

Teacher name: _____

Student name: _____

Category	1	2	3	4
Focus on Topic (Content)	There is one clear, well-focused topic in my writing piece. The main idea stands out and is supported by detailed information.	The main idea in my writing piece is clear but the supporting information is general.	The main idea in my writing piece is somewhat clear but there is a need for more supporting information.	The main idea in my writing piece is not clear. There is a seemingly random collection of information.
Sentence Structure (Sentence Fluency)	All the sentences in my writing piece make sense. They are clear and have complete thoughts.	Most of the sentences in my writing piece make sense. They are clear and have complete thoughts.	Some of the sentences in my writing piece make sense. They are clear and have complete thoughts.	Almost all of the sentences in my writing piece do not make sense. They are not clear and are incomplete thoughts.
Sequencing (Organization)	The details in my writing piece are placed in a logical order—one that makes sense.	Most of the details in my writing piece are placed in a logical order—one that makes sense.	Some of the details in my writing piece are placed in a logical order.	The details in my writing piece are not placed in a logical order.
Grammar & Spelling (Conventions)	I didn't make any grammar or spelling mistakes that distract the reader.	I made 1-2 grammar or spelling mistakes that distract the reader.	I made 3-4 grammar or spelling mistakes that distract the reader.	I made more than 4 grammar or spelling mistakes that distract the reader.
Capitalization & Punctuation (Conventions)	I didn't make any capitalization or punctuation mistakes. Therefore, my story is easy to read.	I made 1 or 2 capitalization or punctuation mistakes, but the story is still easy to read.	I made a few capitalization or punctuation mistakes that catch the reader's attention and make my story more difficult to read.	I made many capitalization or punctuation mistakes that catch the reader's attention and make my story difficult to read.
Penmanship (Conventions)	My paper is neatly written with no distracting corrections.	My paper is neatly written with 1 or 2 distracting corrections (dark cross outs; bumpy white out, words written over, messy erasing).	My writing is readable, but the reader has to make quite a bit of effort to figure out some of the words.	Many words are unreadable OR there are several distracting corrections.

Lesson Plan — Promotional Campaign

Grade: Three

Content objectives: Natural resources; conventions of letter writing; persuasive writing

Information skills objectives: Identify main idea; develop a summary; locate information using a variety of sources; note taking

Technology skills objectives: Use Microsoft Publisher or other software to design and publish a pamphlet; use a word processor to write a final draft of a letter

Time estimate: Five to seven class sessions

Information problem and overarching question: Tell students to pretend that they work for the Bureau of Economic Development for their state. Explain this agency and its importance. Tell the class that the state wants to encourage companies to relocate or open offices in the state to bring in more people and tax dollars. Why are natural resources important to us? What will students need to do? Instruct the class to read in unison the introductory verse for the Big6 Poem. Explain the meaning of the verse.

Big6 #1: Task Definition—What do we need to do?

1. Have the children read in unison the Big6 #1 verse and ask if someone can explain the meaning. Display the Big6 poster and point to Big6 #1. Modify the students' explanation as necessary as you further explain the step.

2. Tell students that they will work in groups to identify the natural resources and other features and landmarks for a state of their choice.

3. Each student will encourage a real or imaginary company to relocate or open a new branch in that state based on the natural resources the company can use. They will make a promotional brochure highlighting the resources and other features and landmarks of the state or communities within the state. Include places of interest that will attract employees with families and state symbols to add appeal and recognition. A letter to the company president persuading him or her to move the company or add a branch will accompany the brochure.

4. Put students in groups of two or three and then have them choose a state. Each group will brainstorm questions it should look up for information about natural resources, features, landmarks, and other places of interest (see Chapter 4). Allow 15 to 20 minutes for the brainstorming session as you monitor progress.

5. Present prepared questions in addition to students' questions.

   a. What are the state's natural resources? (rivers, lakes, other water sources, land use, such as agriculture and cattle grazing, wildlife, native trees, and other plants)

   b. What are the famous landmarks in the state? (mountains, hill country, rivers, lakes, famous buildings and cemeteries, monuments, other structures)

   c. What are the symbols of the state? (bird, song, tree, flower, gemstone, flag, food)

   d. What is the population of the state?

   e. What is the capital city and where is it located? What are other major cities?

Big6 #2: Information Seeking Strategies—What can we use to find what we need?

Read in unison the Big6 #2 verse and ask if someone can explain the meaning. Display the Big6 poster and point to Big6 #2. Modify the students' explanation as necessary as you further explain the step. Tell children that Big6 #2 for their study of a state's natural resources will include identifying the best sources to answer their questions. Use the Process of Exclusion found in Chapter 6 to create a list of sources for the project.

Big6 #3: Location and Access—Where can we find what we need?

Read in unison the Big6 #3 verse and ask if someone can explain the meaning. Display the Big6 poster and point to Big6 #3. Modify the students' explanation as necessary as you further explain the step. Present mini-lessons (see Chapter 6) for each of the skills students will need for accessing resources identified in step two. Consider setting up information stations around the library. Demonstrate process and tips for using each station, or use station helpers as available.

Big6 #4: Use of Information—What information can we use?

Read in unison the Big6 #4 verse and ask if someone can explain the meaning. Display the Big6 poster and point to Big6 #4. Modify the students' explanation as necessary as you further explain the step. Teach steps of the trash and treasure method of note taking (see Chapter 7). Allow ample time (possibly several sessions) for groups to rotate through stations and take notes, actively monitoring groups.

Big6 #5: Synthesis—How can we put our information together?

1. Read in unison the Big6 #5 verse and ask if someone can explain the meaning. Display the Big6 poster and point to Big6 #5. Modify the students' explanation as necessary as you further explain the step.

2. Copy each student's notes and distribute to the other group members for that same state.

3. Each student will encourage a real or imaginary company to relocate or open a new branch in that state or city based on the natural resources the company can use.

4. Students use Microsoft Publisher or construction paper and markers to make a promotional brochure highlighting the resources and other features and landmarks of the state or community, including places of interest that will attract employees with families. Precede the actual construction with a sketch or plan. Instruct students in use of software and design of tri-fold brochures, as appropriate. Students can add the state bird and other symbols to decorate the brochure. Students should include a brief bibliography on the back panel of the brochure.

5. The students will each decide on a real or fictitious company that can benefit from using one or more of the state's natural resources. Care should be taken to assist students in making an appropriate match. The student writes a letter to the company president persuading him or her to locate the company in the state or open a branch. The letter should be taken through the writing process (see the Writing Process Organizer in Appendix F). Academically advanced students can include in their letters ways the state will ensure that the company will not deplete the natural resources.

6. Distribute a scoring guide or rubric for the product and process before students begin on brochure and letter (not included in this plan).

Big6 #6: Evaluation—How will we know if we did well?
Read in unison the Big6 #6 verse and ask if someone can explain the meaning. Display the Big6 poster and point to Big6 #6. Modify the students' explanation as necessary as you further explain the step. Distribute the following individual informal evaluation after students submit their work and complete the scoring guide.

Assessment:
Create rubric or scoring guide for brochure and letter.

Name: _____

1. What did I learn?

2. What skill did I learn that I can use again?

3. How can I use it?

4. Did my brochure and letter follow the guidelines on the scoring guide?

5. What could I do better next time?

6. Did I include the information I found out about my subject?

7. Which sources did I find useful?

8. Which sources did I need but did not have?

9. What did I contribute to my group?

10. What did I like most about doing this project?

11. I think my grade will be _____ because

_____.

CHAPTER 11
Literature Appreciation, Storytelling, and the Big6

Guiding Questions

- How can teachers and library media specialists use the Big6 to support genre studies?
- How can the Big6 support author studies?
- How can teachers and library media specialists use the Big6 to feature children's book awards?
- How can teachers and children use the Big6 to tell stories?

Whether in the classroom or school library media center, reading aloud to children and having them respond to literature instills a love of reading at an early age as well as satisfies many state academic standards. Incorporating activities into read-aloud sessions that support the curriculum and extend children's thinking and creative expression while integrating the information search process makes good sense.

Consider the following idea when beginning to integrate the Big6 into story time: As you are reading aloud, stop and have students use the Big6 to help storybook characters solve their problems. Take the class through each step of the process as soon as the problem is encountered in the story. Have pairs or individuals tell the class how they would solve the problem. Finish reading the story, ask the class which solutions they enjoyed, and compare their ideas to those of the author.

The additional activities below will satisfy many state and district curriculum standards in literature appreciation, listening skills, and oral expression while exciting and engaging early elementary school children.

Literature Studies through Read Aloud

Biographies

Reading aloud biographies of notable persons may not be high on the list of genre that teachers and library media specialists enjoy sharing with young children. Promoting biographies during story time should encourage children to choose one for pleasure reading. Introduce children to biographies on President's Day or a notable person's birthday or special event. Free or subscription database searches on the Internet will produce many resources to find holidays that you can connect to notable persons. Beginning in second and third grades, children's interest in other people and in history begins to surface as they move into the operational stage of cognitive development. Kindergartners and first graders can enjoy simple biographies about very well-known people whose names they may encounter.

Many publishers have picture books about notable people. Holiday House's series, *Picture Book Biographies* by David A. Adler, offers simple text and illustrations in a 32-page, easy-to-read narrative format quite suitable for reading aloud to kindergartners, first graders, or second graders. ABDO Publishing Company's *Checkerboard Biography Series* presents in a 32-page book illustrations, photographs, tables, maps, fact pages, timeline, table of contents, and index. The actual text, while lengthier, covers 25 pages, and it is suitable for reading aloud second and third graders. Picture Window Books biography series of famous Americans offers 24 pages of text including a glossary, index, timelines, and fun facts. Check your school library for other biographies suitable for young listeners.

The teacher or library media specialist can begin by asking children what they know about the type of books called "biographies." Record the children's responses. Show several biographies and read the titles asking children if they have heard of the notable people. Tell the class that biographies are accounts of events that make up a person's life, usually written in a book but also written as a script for television or movies. They will learn about biographies and will use the Big6 to help find out what authors include in a complete biography.

Consider using puppets and singing (see Chapter 10) to help introduce the Big6 steps. Display the steps of the Big6 so students see each step as it is introduced and can keep track of their progress though the process.

What makes an enjoyable biography?

Big6 #1: What do we need to do? Tell the class that they will learn about what makes an enjoyable and complete biography.

Big6 #2: What can we use to find what we need? Ask students what they think should be included in a story of someone's life—in other words, what would they like to know about a person? Also, what makes a book enjoyable to hear or read? Record student responses and add any others as needed. What could help them find this information? Tell students that you will use books to help them figure out what information is interesting and what may be missing.

Big6 #3: Where can we find what we need? Demonstrate the use of the library's catalog to find biographies. Show students how the call number on the catalog record matches those on the actual book and helps readers find it on the shelf. Some libraries have biographies in a separate section while others shelve them according to the person's occupation, ethnicity, or other reason. Choose three or four biographies to read in separate read-aloud sessions. If possible, select those that reflect the cultures and ethnicities of the students in the class. A 32-page book will keep students' attention and allow you to finish in one session. Before reading each biography, show children the table of contents, and index, if present, in the book.

Big6 #4: What information can we use? For each book read, instruct students to listen for the type of information that is included about each person. Write "What makes a biography?" on a chart tablet page or other large display. Read short sections, stopping to ask students what kind of information they heard. If a student replies that the notable person moved from Kentucky to Indiana when she was small, record "about her childhood" on the note taking form. Include also the components that make a good story: lively verbs and adjectives (or lively words) and good illustrations that extend and support the text. Continue recording notes for each section of the book, as well as citing the title and author at the end of the book. Repeat the note taking process for several biographies of various notable figures.

Big6 #5: How can we put our information together?
Make the following comparison chart (Figure 11.1) using the recorded notes, placing in the top row those categories the class identified. Use the chart to record the elements of the subsequent biographies. Place a checkmark in the appropriate box for the elements identified in each book. Summarize by asking the class which categories are included in every book. As an extension, developmentally ready students or classes can write a biography of a parent, grandparent, teacher, notable town leader, or school principal, integrating the criteria on the chart with the writing process (see Appendix F for the Writing Process Organizer).

Figure 11.1 Example Biography Comparison Chart

Notable person's name	Childhood	Education	Careers	Significant contributions	Interesting facts and stories	Written using lively verbs and interesting adjectives	Pictures add to story
Abraham Lincoln	✓	✓	✓	✓			
George Washington	✓	✓	✓	✓	✓	✓	✓
Barbara Jordon	✓	✓	✓	✓		✓	

Big6 #6: How will we know if we did well?

Read an additional biography and have students use the chart to determine if it meets the criteria of one that is enjoyable and well-constructed. Compare original biographies to the chart to ensure that all components are included.

Animal Stories

Can animals really talk? Can they eat with a fork at the table? After reading an animal story, use the Big6 to check the facts. Help the class change parts of the story to reflect only the facts of animal behavior. Do they still enjoy the story? Second and third graders can work in groups to rewrite sections using what they find out about authentic animal behavior. Conduct a class discussion about why authors give animals human behaviors.

Author Studies

Library media specialists love to introduce children to authors who will quickly become their favorites. The Big6 is the perfect process for studying the author and his or her body of work. After reading two or three books by a single author (ex. Marc Brown), ask students how the books are alike and different and tell what they already know about Marc Brown. (Here, you may want to construct a KWL chart. See Chapter 4.) "What other books has he written that we would enjoy? Let's use the Big6 to find out about Marc Brown."

Allow children to offer suggestions and brainstorm as appropriate for each of the steps (see Chapters 4 through 9 for additional strategies). Of course, the examples below are simply suggestions—the students and library media specialist will include their ideas for each of the steps.

Big6 #1: Task Definition—What do we need to do?

Find out about Marc Brown. What do we want to know about him? Examples of questions children may add:

- How old is he?
- How many books has he written?
- Where does he get his ideas?
- Are any of his characters made from real people?
- Does he illustrate all of his books?
- Where does he live?
- Did he have pets when he was little?
- What else is interesting about Marc Brown?

Big6 #2: Information Seeking Strategies—What can we use to find what we need?

Web sites, book cover flaps, other books about authors.

Big6 #3: Location and Access—Where can we find what we need?

Online catalog (use this opportunity to introduce author and subject searching to second and third graders and explain when they will use each); search engine such as Google, or Answers.com; subject directory, such as subscription-based *netTrekker* or *KidsClick* available for free at <http://kidsclick.org>.

Big6 #4: Use of Information—What information can we use?

Choose a note taking method for whole or small group (see Chapter 7). For younger students, whole group note taking will work best. Capable second and third graders can work in small groups, each group finding answers to a subset of the questions.

Big6 #5: Synthesis—How can we put our information together?

Small groups can present their information to the class. Review the "answers" to the questions and read additional Marc Brown books to the class over a period of several sessions. If the author has an email address or another method for contact, have students write a class letter to him posing more questions and observations about the books. They can also include ideas for additional books they would like for him to write.

Big6 #6: Evaluation—How will we know if we did well?

Did we find the answers to our questions? Was our letter as good as we could make it? Do we want to continue reading books by Marc Brown?

Award Winners

The Randolph Caldecott Medal

Over several weekly story time sessions, read books from the Caldecott Medal award list available <http://ala.org/ala/mgrps/divs/alsc/awardsgrants/bookmedia/caldecottmedal/caldecottmedal.cfm>. Ask students what they like about the books and what they all have in common. Show the medal on each book and read the words: The Caldecott Medal. Ask if anyone knows what it means for a book to win this award. "What do you notice about the illustrations, or pictures, in the stories?" Allow time for students to give their observations. Then say, "Let's find out more about The Caldecott Medal by using the Big6." Take students through each of the steps referring to the Big6 poster (see Appendix A). Allow children to provide ideas for each of the steps, then fill in sources and information as needed (see Chapters 4 through 9 for additional strategies). Sing or say the Big6 Song or Poem before each step (see Chapter 10).

Time frame: Three to five sessions for Big6 sequence, after librarian spends several weeks reading books from the award list.

Prepare: Note taking organizer (see Chapter 7 for appropriate format), chart for class to fill in after notes are taken in Big6 #4, materials for designing class award.

Big6 #1: Task Definition—What do we need to do?

- Find out about the Caldecott Medal and why some books win it.
- How did the medal get its name?
- Who is Caldecott?
- What did Caldecott do to get the medal named after him or her?
- When did it start?
- Who sponsors (is responsible for) the award?
- How many books have won the award?
- Do only books for children win the award?
- How do they choose the books that win the award?
- Is there a second place?
- Are there interesting facts about the award?

Big6 #2: Information Seeking Strategies—What can we use to find what we need?

Encyclopedias, Web sites, and Caldecott posters.

Big6 #3: Location and Access—Where can we find what we need?

Library shelf and computer, search engines, such as Google, Ask, or Answers.com, and the library wall for Caldecott poster.

Big6 #4: Use of Information—What information can we use?

Take notes from sources, answering the questions identified in Big6 #1 (see Chapter 7 for note taking strategies).

Big6 #5: Synthesis—How can we put our information together?

Tell students that only one book and two honor books win each year. However, many others have beautiful and engaging illustrations. They should design and name a medal that their class will award to a picture book. (This may be done in small groups). Using the notes, create a chart by which students can compare other picture books (see Figure 11.2) and have students nominate books for the new class award.

Big6 #6: Evaluation—How will we know if we did well?

The class will vote on a book to which they will award their class medal. The criteria will be the same or similar to that of the Caldecott Award. Of course, the class can change any of the criteria, choosing to award illustrators from outside the U.S. or from past years, for example. Activity can span over a period of several weeks or months, as children read and nominate books. Students can write and share persuasive book reports, presenting using available technology, why their book of choice should be included. They can also nominate from those which the library media specialist reads to the whole class.

Figure 11.2 Example of Caldecott Chart for Class Award

Class Medal Award (based on the Caldecott Award)	Picture book for children	Artist is the illustrator or co-illustrators	Illustrations are distinguished (beautiful, excellent, like no other)	Original work (not put together from other sources or reprinted)	Published in last year	Resident of the United States	Written in English
Picture book title 1	✓	✓	✓				
Picture book title 2	✓		✓		✓		✓
Picture book title 3	✓		✓	✓		✓	

Coretta Scott King Author Award and Coretta Scott King Illustrator Award

With engaging stories and illustrations, books that won the Coretta Scott King Author and Illustrator Awards will delight children during story time sessions and offer a unique opportunity to introduce or review the Big6 as children learn about the awards. A list of winners is available at <http://www.ala.org/ala/mgrps/rts/emiert/cskbookawards/index.cfm>. Not all of the Author Award books are suitable for reading aloud to primary-age students due to their length and content, but there are more than enough picture books in both categories to interest children for many weeks. Consider using the same activities in Big6 #1 through Big6 #4 as the Caldecott Award (see page 145). Questions that the class will ask for Big6 #1 may include:

- Who was Coretta Scott King?
- What did she do to get the medal named after her?
- When did the award start?
- Why are there two awards? (here the library media specialist may discuss the Coretta Scott King/John Steptoe Award for New Talent—a third award!)
- Who sponsors (is responsible for) the award?
- How many books have won the award?
- How do they choose the books that win the awards?
- Is there a second place?
- Are there interesting facts about the award?

Library media specialists will need to paraphrase and simplify some of the criteria so their young audience will understand it. For the final product and evaluation, the class can create its own cultural award based on the criteria for the Coretta Scott King Author and Illustrator awards (see Figure 11.3).

Figure 11.3 Example of Coretta Scott King Awards Chart for Class Cultural Award

Class medal award for author or illustrator (Based on Coretta Scott King Author and Illustrator Awards)	Shows some aspect of the African American experience—past, present, or future	Is written/illustrated by an African American	Should make the reader think and appreciate beauty and be of highest quality	Includes characters who learn and develop, is accurate and understandable by the age for which it was written	Published in last year	Written for a youth audience	Original work
Book title 1	✓	✓	✓				
Book title 2	✓	✓	✓		✓		✓
Book title 3	✓		✓	✓	✓	✓	✓

Oral Storytelling

(Reprinted from *The Big6 Newsletter*, Vol. 1, No. 6, July/August, Linworth Publishing, Inc., 1998.)

"Toad was hopping along the hot desert sand looking for a cool place to get out of the heat. She was looking for a home to stay in when the sun was too hot for her bumpy skin. She needed a home that was not too hot, not too hard, and not too prickly."

The first graders listened intently as the bumpy green toad puppet defined her task. As the story developed, the students sang along with Toad and learned about the homes of various desert animals as the librarian taped a picture of each animal (see Figure 11.4) and its home on a white board. They laughed and clapped for Toad when she finally solved her problem.

Using a poster with the Big6 in question form, the library media specialist explained to the students how Toad used the process to solve her information problem.

Big6 #1: What do I need to do?
Toad needs a new home that cannot be too hot, too hard, or too prickly.

Big6 #2: What can I use to find what I need?
She can either look for one herself or ask one of the other desert animals. She decides to ask other desert animals.

Big6 #3: Where can I find what I need?
She walks until she sees Javelina.
She walks until she sees Lizard.
She walks until she sees Pack Rat.
She keeps walking until she decides to dig a hole in the sand.

Big6 #4: What information can I use?
She asks Javelina about his home and decides that it is too hot. Javelina tells her to find a cooler place with more water.
She asks Lizard about his home and decides that it is too hard, and Lizard tells her to find a place that is softer.
She asks Pack Rat about his home and decides that it is too prickly, and Pack Rat tells her to find a smoother home.

Big6 #5: How can I put my information together?
She finds that the animals' homes are not suitable for her and uses what they tell her to find a home deep in the sand under the yucca plant.

Big6 #6: How will I know if I did well?
She knows it is good because it is not too hot, not too hard, and not too prickly, and she remembers the song.

With parent helpers, groups of three students placed story strips onto chart paper into the Big6 sequence referring to the white board for the order of the animals. They easily understood how Toad had to revisit Big6 #3 and Big6 #4 several times before she found a place to live.

Using the Big6, the teacher and library media specialist discussed each step of the ensuing desert animal study with the students and their parent helpers. Parents would help their groups locate information about a specific desert animal (a physical description and where it lives in the desert) and draw a picture of the animal in its habitat for a class book. Students wrote a sentence explaining why its home would or would not be suitable for Toad. When the teacher read the completed book to the class, the library media specialist administered a simple written evaluation instrument for each student to complete. The student evaluations proved that they thoroughly enjoyed the process—"I liked the toad and the big six and I love desert animals" wrote one first grader.

Figure 11.4 Animals Used in "A Home for Toad"

A Home for Toad:
The Story

by: Barbara A. Jansen

Toad was hopping along the hot desert sand. She was looking for a cool place to get out of the heat. She wanted a home to stay in when the sun was too hot for her bumpy skin. She needed a home that was not too hot, not too hard, and not too prickly. She thought about where she would find out about homes that were not too hot, not too hard, and not too prickly. She knew she could look for one for herself or ask other animals. She decided to ask other animals. So she set off in search of other desert animals to help her find a home that was not too hot, not too hard, and not too prickly.

By and by, she found Javelina scampering in and out of mesquite trees, digging for roots and singing a catchy little tune: "I'm happy, happy, happy as I can be because my home of mesquite is just right for me. "I'm happy, happy, happy as I can be!"

Toad liked that tune and wanted to learn it. She asked Javelina about her home and Javelina told her that it suited her perfectly—it was in a sandy hot place to dig for roots, it had some shade to rest in, but it was nice and hot most of the time. Toad told Javelina that she was looking for a home that was not too hot, not too hard, and not too prickly.

Javelina's home was too hot. Javelina told Toad to find a home that was cooler and that had more water. Toad then asked Javelina to teach her the song. After a number of practice tries, Toad thought she had the song in her head. As soon as she hopped out of sight of Javelina, Toad tried to sing the song "I'm happy, happy, happy…" but found that she had forgotten the words. She tried and tried to remember the words to that nice song that Javelina taught her when she saw Lizard and heard him singing the same song, but a little differently:

"I'm happy, happy, happy as I can be because my home of rock is just right for me. I'm happy, happy, happy as I can be." Toad liked that tune and wanted to learn it. She asked Lizard about his home and Lizard told her that it suited him perfectly: it was in a hard place to take a nice nap in the sun, it had some shade for him to get out of the sun when it got too hot, and it was nice and flat. Toad told Lizard that she was looking for a home that was not too hot, not too hard, and not too prickly. Lizard's home was too hard. Lizard told her to find a home that was softer. Toad then asked Lizard to teach her the song. After a number of practice tries, Toad thought she had the song in her head.

As soon as Toad hopped out of sight of Lizard, she tried to sing the song:

"I'm happy, happy, happy…" but had forgotten the words. Toad tried and tried to remember the words to that nice song that Lizard taught her when she saw Pack Rat and heard him singing the same song, but a little differently: "I'm happy, happy, happy as I can be because my home of cactus is just right for me. I'm happy, happy, happy as I can be." Toad liked that tune and wanted to learn it. She asked Pack Rat about her home and Pack Rat told her that it suited her perfectly: it had a nice place to store things, it had some holes to sleep in, and it stored water to drink. Toad told Pack Rat that she was looking for a home that was not too hot, not too hard, and not too prickly. Pack Rat's home was too prickly. Pack Rat told her to find a home that was smoother. Toad then asked Pack Rat to teach her the song. After a number of practice tries, Toad thought she had the song in her head.

As soon as she hopped out of sight of Pack Rat, Toad tried to sing the song: "I'm happy, happy, happy…" but had forgotten the words. This was just too much for Toad. The sun was beating down on her bumpy back, she needed water to drink, and she needed a nice place to rest. To make matters worse, she could not remember the words to that nice song that the other animals kept singing.

"Javelina told me to find a place that was cool and had more water, Lizard told me to find a place that was softer, and Pack Rat told me to find a place that was smoother." Toad thought about the nice sand under a yucca plant. She dug and dug in the sand until she had buried herself quite deep. The earth was cool under the yucca plant. There was water to drink in the moisture of the roots. And, there were nice fat worms and grubs to eat as she dug deeper in the sand.

"This is nice! It is not too hot, not too hard, and not too prickly. I think I have found my home underneath the desert floor, thanks to my friends' advice." "I'm happy, happy, happy as I can be because my home of sand is just right for me. I'm happy, happy, happy as I can be."

Story and song based upon the book, Lizard's Song *by George Shannon (Greenwillow Books, 1981).*

Considerations for Choosing Appropriate Stories

Children respond enthusiastically to stories and relating them to the Big6 research process allows for easier understanding and meaningful instruction. In choosing or creating stories to use, teachers and library media specialists should consider these factors: the characters must have a problem to solve requiring information for the solution; students must be given a curriculum connection as a reason to use the Big6; and the story should have action, use puppets or other visuals, or encourage audience participation, keeping the learner motivated and responsive.

Strategies for Implementation

Teachers and library media specialists can use several strategies to successfully integrate stories into the Big6 process and subject-area curriculum:

1. Read a children's picture book that has the appropriate curriculum connection. For example, when studying the characteristics of amphibians, the library media specialist introduced the lesson by reading Ted Arnold's *Green Wilma* (Dial Books for Young Readers, 1993). The toad puppet held by the library media specialist became confused by the little girl who turned into a frog. This led to a conversation between the puppet and the library media specialist, concluding with a problem to solve: find out about what makes one animal an amphibian and another one a human. The library media specialist asked, "What process can we use to help us find the solution to our problem? The Big6!" The library media specialist had the puppet sing the Big6 Song when beginning an activity for each step (see Chapter 10). Of course, children's literature can be used without puppets and singing. The library media specialist and teacher will need to make the curriculum and Big6 connection however, through discussion with the class.

2. Modify a story from a children's book. The idea for "A Home for Toad," (see accompanying story) came from the lively story *Lizard's Song* by George Shannon (Greenwillow Books, 1981). A silly bear likes the song that lizard sings but cannot remember the words until he finds a place of his own. If the character has a problem to solve, the story can usually be modified to the Big6.

3. Write a story based on the curriculum connection. When studying the lives of cowboys, the library media specialist made up a story about a little girl who wished to be a cowgirl but wasn't sure what she needed to know about cowboys/girls in order to get a job on a ranch. The story took her through the information-finding process which included some interesting and funny adventures, until she finally decided that being a cowgirl was hard work. She decided to become a computer programmer or brain surgeon instead!

(The first graders didn't quite appreciate the ending to the story, but it elicited some laughs from the teachers!) The library media specialist used a large poster of the Big6 to show the students how the girl had used the Big6 process to solve her problem. The teacher and library media specialist introduced the assignment to the students (learn about the life of a cowboy to determine what makes it so difficult). They took them step by step through the process.

4. Use extemporaneous dialog with puppets. Upon arriving in the library second grade students were met by a glum and grumpy Maybelle the cow puppet. She could not understand what the big deal was about that silly nursery rhyme that mothers taught their little children. The library media specialist had the second graders recite "Hey diddle, diddle" with Maybelle interrupting at the part about the cow jumping over the moon: "Stop! I can't stand it! Why would a self-respecting cow want to go to the moon so far away when there is nice grass to munch on and great books to read right here in the (name of school here) library? I just cannot stand the thought of it! The very nerve!"

The library media specialist asked Maybelle how she could make such a determination about the moon if she didn't know anything about it. She suggested that Maybelle find out about the moon before she make such a harsh decision.

"How can I find out about the moon?" asked Maybelle. "Well," said the library media specialist...

5. Encourage children to use the Big6 to invent their own stories. They can use the Writing Process Organizer (see Appendix F) to plan and write a complete story. Or, they can plan the story and simply tell it orally instead of formally recording it. With guidance, children can use the storytelling organizer on the following page to develop an oral story.

Using the Big6 to Develop an Oral Story

List your characters here: _____

_____

_____

Who is the main character? _____

Where does the story take place? _____

_____

When does the story take place? _____

_____

Big6 #1: What problem does the main character or other characters have?
What do the characters need to do to solve the problem?

_____

_____

Big6 #2: What or who can the characters use to help them solve the problem?

_____

_____

Big6 #3: Where can the characters find the help they need?

_____

_____

Big6 #4: How can the characters use the sources to help solve the problem?

_____

_____

Big6 #5: How can the characters show how they solved their problem?

_____

_____

Big6 #6: How will the characters know if they solved their problem successfully?

_____

_____

How does the story end?

_____

_____

When you tell your story, you do not need to say each Big6 number.
Simply tell the story like you would enjoy hearing it!

Sharing Stories

Have a storytelling week in the library to feature those students who want to perform in front of an audience, inviting other classes to listen. Children can illustrate the stories they create or make props for the storytelling session. Consider having students record into a microphone on the computer and save the stories as sound files. If the school has the available technology and expertise, make the stories into podcasts for others to hear, giving students a wider and more authentic audience. Consider using Animoto <http://animoto.com>, Microsoft Photo Story <http://www.microsoft.com/windowsxp/using/digitalphotography/PhotoStory/default.mspx>, or other digital storytelling programs. Children may enjoy sending, with teacher guidance and parent approval, their stories via the Internet to parents and grandparents.

Using storytelling with the Big6 motivates young learners to stay focused on the project from Big6 #1 to the very last word on their Big6 #6 self-evaluations. You'll have just as much fun finding and creating the stories and designing instruction that will make children love the information problem-solving process!

CHAPTER 12
Using the Big6 to Learn about the School Library

Guiding Questions

- Can the Big6 help kindergartners and first graders learn how to take care of books?
- How can students learn how the shelves are arranged in the school library for finding books of personal interest or for information needs?
- How can primary-age learners use the Big6 to connect them to the nonfiction section of their school library?

Learning about the school library remains a large part of the curriculum for library media specialists working with primary-age students. Often scheduled classes will come to the library for a weekly session and to check out books. Library media specialists use this time for reading aloud and "library" instruction. They strive to connect the scheduled library time to a particular grade level's course of study and integrate the essential information and communications technology skills into the subject-area curriculum. However, stand-alone instruction on the organization of the library and other library-related lessons may be necessary when collaboration and integration do not fit into the schedule. The following ideas will help library media specialists plan for effective use of that time. Using the Big6 to introduce young learners to their school library will help them transfer the process as needed for their curricular units of study.

Caring for Books and the Big6

On the first day of school, kindergartners come into the library looking for their missing gingerbread man. They ask the library media specialist if she has seen it. She takes the class to the picture book section and pulls *The Gingerbread Man* by Paul Galdone off the shelf. "Is this it?" she asks. "No, it is not a book, it is a gingerbread man!" the class shouts. The library media specialist explains to the children that they can find books about the gingerbread man in the library, but the actual gingerbread man must be somewhere else, maybe in the nurse's office. She tells the students that they may choose a book from a bin to keep in the classroom, taking it home only after they learn more about the library. After each child selects a book and checks it out, the class walks to the nurse's office, holding their books as the library media specialist previously demonstrated.

During subsequent library visits, the library media specialist reads to and shows the kindergartners proper library procedures and book care, allowing the children to take books home after a few weeks of housing them in the classroom. Using a puppet for each library session, the library media specialist gains the children's trust and affection. The children respond well to the character and believe what it has to say. The puppet uses the Big6 to learn how to take care of books so that it can take one home. The activity sequence can take one or more days depending on how long you have for each session.

Scenario: After a two or three weeks of checking out books and leaving them in the classroom, Celestine the toad puppet whines to the library media specialist about wanting to take her library book home so that her mother can read it to her. The library media specialist expresses to Celestine her fear about having the nice library book getting damaged in the pond from water or the algae she eats. Celestine says, "I see your point. The water will ruin the whole book and the algae and bugs will make a big mess on the pages. Well, how should I take care of the book? If I learn how and promise that I'll follow the rules, can I take it home?"

The library media specialist agrees and suggests that they use the Big6 to learn about how to take care of books. "After all, that is what the older kids use when they need information, so there is no reason why we shouldn't use it, too!" At this point, she shows the Big6 poster and teaches Celestine and the class the Big6 Song and has the children and puppet join her in singing the refrain. She sings the appropriate verse for each of the following steps:

Big6 #1: Task Definition—What do we need to do?

Tell the class they will learn how to take care of library books so they can take them home. Say, "We will find the answers to these questions about how to take care of books":

- Where should you put your book when you are taking it home or bringing it back to school?

- What things at home might harm books?
- How can we keep these harmful things away from our books?
- Where should we keep our books when we are at home?"

Big6 #2: Information Seeking Strategies—What can we use to find what we need?

Ask the class, "Who or what could help us answer our questions?" and get them to offer suggestions, such as the library assistant (if the school employs one, of course), the principal, the nurse, or the secretary. The class can use what it knows about taking care of books, or it can look at how a book is made and decide what would be the best way to care for it.

Big6 #3: Location and Access—Where can we find what we need?

In the library and office.

Big6 #4: Use of Information—What information can we use?

Invite the helpers identified in Big6 #2 into the library or take the class to them. Have students ask the questions and record the answers on a large chart tablet under each person's name. Optional: demonstrate the effects of water, food, and markers, on paper.

Big6 #5: Synthesis—How can we put our information together?

- Read the answers from all the helpers and ask children which ones they think are the best. Make a list of "Book Care Guidelines (or Rules)" on a clean piece of chart paper or poster board. Have students "read" the list aloud with Celestine the puppet. Ask students to act out the rules as you say each one. Give scenarios and ask students what they would do, such as: "What should you do if your little brother wants to read your book?" "Should you read your book in the bathtub?"
- "If you want to read your book while you are eating breakfast, what care should you take?"
- "Should you take your book to Grandma's house?"
- "What should you do if your book accidentally gets torn or dirty?"
- "When should you bring your book back to school?"

Big6 #6: Evaluation—How will we know if we did well?

Say to the class, "If we bring our book back on time and it is not damaged, our librarian will allow us to take another book home."

Arrangement of the School Library

While shelf arrangement technically falls under Big6 #3 *Location and Access*, library media specialists often teach this skill out of context due to the limited time they have to integrate the skill into the content-area curriculum. And, students also need to use their school library to find books of interest to read for pleasure, usually before they will use it for information-searching for a class project.

Starting in the late spring, kindergartners can learn how to find books by their favorite authors in the picture book section. First graders should be ready as soon as they enter school. They can learn how to find nonfiction books of interest, and second and third graders can learn to use the online catalog to find specific books in nonfiction. Of course, not all students fit these timelines and some will be ready long before their classmates, while others will need to wait even longer as they mature cognitively.

Finding Picture Books by the First Letter of the Author's Name

Over the span of several weeks, read aloud a variety of alphabet books to kindergartners or first graders. Ask the students what the books have in common. Tell students that we use letters for a several reasons, such as making words and putting things in order. Continue conversing with the students: "What would happen if during the night a big wind came into the library and blew all the books in a pile on the floor? We wouldn't be able to find the books we need without a lot of work digging through the piles. The alphabet is one way books are organized in the library so we can easily find those that we enjoy. Let's find out how the alphabet helps us find books."

Time frame: Three class periods

Prepare: Large poster of spine label from a fictional picture book; plain index cards or paper, enough for each child to have one; markers or crayons, one for each child

Day 1:

1. Adhere the spine label poster on the board or wall. Read the picture book for which you made the spine label.

2. Show the students the author's name and then show the spine label. Tell them that it is the same label as the large label on the board or wall.

3. Write the author's name next to the spine label. Ask students what they notice about the label and the author's name. They should say that some of the letters are the same, or they may need to be prompted.

4. Circle the letters in the author's last name and the corresponding letters on the spine label.

5. Take the students to the shelf where the book would be found and point to the letter that corresponds to the name (if the shelves in the picture book section are labeled with letters).

6. Tell students that during the next session, they will learn where a book that they write would be on the shelf.

Day 2:

1. Repeat steps 1 through 4 of Day 1 using a different picture book.
2. Hand out index cards and markers.
3. Tell students to write their first name on the card. Now write their last name. Some students may need help writing and spelling their names.
4. Have students circle the first letter of their last name.
5. Tell the students to turn over their cards and write a large E at the top (model). Then they should write the first letter of their last name under the E (model).
6. Take up cards and tell students that they will find where their name would be on the shelf the next time they come to the library.

Day 3:

1. Repeat steps 1 through 4 from Day 1 using a different picture book.
2. Hand out the students' cards.
3. Tell students that they should go to the letter on the shelf that is the same as the letter in their last name. Instruct the students to stand and wait for you (and any adult helpers you can find) to check to see if they found the right place.
4. When they have found their letter, take their card and tell them that they can choose a book to take home from that section.

Day 4 (optional for the spring of first grade and second grade):

1. Repeat steps 1 through 4 from Day 1 using a different picture book.
2. Hand out the cards to students. Instruct them to add the second and third letters of their last names to the first letter (model).
3. Have students find the exact place on the picture book shelf where they would find their own name. They should place their card in the spot.
4. Check for accuracy and re-teach as needed.

Repeat these steps throughout the year as needed for review. Change the type of books, adding novels (chapter books) with second and third graders. Extend the learning by giving students index card-sized "spine labels" of their favorite authors and have them find these on the shelves.

Shelf Arrangement for Dewey Decimal Classification

Emerging and new readers are intensely interested in drawing books, snakes, dogs and cats, cars, robots, and any number of nonfiction topics. Introducing students to these sections gives them a greater variety in their choices and prepares them to find books for informational needs as defined by the curriculum. The Dewey Decimal Classification system (DDC) can intimidate even the boldest adult—there are jokes made at its expense!—so demystifying it at an early age will go a long way in nurturing life-long library users.

Young learners will not understand the Dewey system, as it is abstract, including seemingly random numbers that represent all subjects. A general understanding of classification will help children locate a variety of interesting books.

Kindergarten and first grade: Ask students to tell everything they know about the grocery store. Continue, "What if your father wants only to buy a carton of milk? How does he find it? Does he have to search every shelf in the store to find the milk? No, he goes to the section called dairy where there is milk, butter, yogurt, pudding, and other products that contain milk and need refrigeration. What are some other sections of the grocery store? The library is arranged in a similar manner, except it does not have dairy, vegetables, or meat, but topics like animals, drawing books, sports, and story books. What other topics do you enjoy doing or reading about?"

Take students around the library and point out the sections in which they have interest (animals, folktales, etc.). Show them a selection of picture-type books they may enjoy from the nonfiction section. Explaining to young children that the nonfiction section has books about "real" things may be confusing, as the shelves also store folktales, fairy tales, poetry, and other types of literature. Even picture books and novels are technically in the 813 section. However, because there are so many, we put those classes in their own section, usually labeling them with an E or F. In my experience, introducing the youngest learners to those Dewey sections with popular topics, without labeling them as such, excited children and broadened their choices without confusion. Simple signage or pictures on popular sections will help youngsters locate books of interest.

Second and third grade: While a deep knowledge of the Dewey Decimal system may not serve 7 to 9-year-old children well, an introduction to the general numbering system will help them find books for personal interest and informational needs. An Internet search of "Dewey Decimal" and "kids" returns several sites that attempt to list the classifications for students, most that will help those in upper elementary to high school due to the immature developmental level of young learners.

The Online Computer Library Center (OCLC), which owns DDC, has an interactive tutorial <http://oclc.org/dewey/resources/tour/> aimed at children that teaches the 10 classifications and more. While engagingly using flash technology, most of the tutorial will be out of reach intellectually for 8 and 9-year-old children. By carefully choosing and matching sections with individual learners, library media specialists can use parts of the tutorial effectively.

Thinkquest, sponsored by the Oracle Education Foundation, offers a tutorial "Do We Really Know Dewey" <http://library.thinkquest.org/5002/index.shtml>, which aims to help young learners understand the basic concept of the classification system. However, the abstract nature of the system renders it difficult to teach and learn. A library media specialist can use this site to help her second and third graders learn the system, taking care to match each section with ready students, as not all will grasp the concepts.

Creating original DDC activities, as well as using specific Internet resources, to introduce second and third graders to the numbered section of the library may serve young students best. I introduced three or four sections during consecutive library visits. During each session I displayed on the white board, the numbers (300, 400, 500 for example) and discussed, one at a time, what each number represents and showed interesting and obvious books from that section. The students toured those sections observing and listening to the additional titles I pulled from the shelves. I then handed out one of the books to each child and had the children walk to the section in which their book would "live."

In subsequent sessions, the library media specialist can explain the numbers on spine labels and help the children understand how the books are arranged on the shelf. Young children understand that a call number is like the address of their house, so the "address" of the book is where it "lives" on the shelf. The call number on the spine label is like the address on an envelope that comes in the mail.

Read a 24 or 32-page book about an animal, visually and orally explaining the call number on the spine label to the class (see Figure 12.1). Distribute slips of paper with simple call numbers to pairs of students, instructing them to find the general area where they would find that number. Repeat this activity periodically until each student successfully locates the section on the shelf where the call number is found.

Figure 12.1 Explanation of Call Number on Spine Label

5 = Natural Science (500)
59 = Animals (590)
597 = Cold-blooded vertebrates (animals with backbones)
597.9 = Reptiles
597.96 = Snakes

SMI = the first three letters of the author's last name

Appendix A Primary Poster

The Big6™

1. What do we need to do?

2. What can we use to find what we need?

I know!

3. Where can we find what we need?

4. What information can we use?

5. How can we show what we learned?

6. How will we know if we did well?

Big6 copyright 1987, Eisenberg & Berkowitz. Poster text and design by Barbara A. Jansen.

Appendix B Primary Poster in Spanish

The Big6™

1. ¿Qué tenemos que hacer?

2. ¿Qué podemos utilizar para encontrar lo que necesitamos?

I know!

3. ¿Dónde podemos encontrar lo que necesitamos?

4. ¿Qué información podemos utilizar?

5. ¿Cómo podemos demostrar lo que hemos aprendido?

6. ¿Cómo sabremos si lo hicimos bien?

Big6 copyright 1987, Eisenberg & Berkowitz. Poster text and design by Barbara A. Jansen.
Spanish translation by Malia LeMond.

Appendix C Bookmarks

 1. What do we need to do?

2. What can we use to find what we need?

 3. Where can we find what we need?

 4. What information can we use?

 5. How can we show what we learned?

 6. How will we know if we did well?

Big6© Eisenberg and Berkowitz, 1987.
Design by B. Jansen, 2007.

 1. What do we need to do?

2. What can we use to find what we need?

 3. Where can we find what we need?

 4. What information can we use?

 5. How can we show what we learned?

 6. How will we know if we did well?

Big6© Eisenberg and Berkowitz, 1987.
Design by B. Jansen, 2007.

Appendix D Spanish Bookmarks

1.¿Qué tenemos que hacer?

2.¿Qué podemos utilizar para encontrar lo que necesitamos?

I know !

3.¿Dónde podemos encontrar lo que necesitamos?

4. ¿Qué información podemos utilizar?

5. ¿Cómo podemos demostrar lo que hemos aprendido?

6. ¿Cómo sabremos si lo hicimos bien?

Big6© Eisenberg and Berkowitz, 1987.
Design by B. Jansen, 2007.
Spanish translation by Malia LeMond.

1.¿Qué tenemos que hacer?

2.¿Qué podemos utilizar para encontrar lo que necesitamos?

I know !

3.¿Dónde podemos encontrar lo que necesitamos?

4. ¿Qué información podemos utilizar?

5. ¿Cómo podemos demostrar lo que hemos aprendido?

6. ¿Cómo sabremos si lo hicimos bien?

Big6© Eisenberg and Berkowitz, 1987.
Design by B. Jansen, 2007.
Spanish translation by Malia LeMond.

Research Journal

Draw a Picture of Your Topic Here.⤴

My Topic: _____

My Name: _____

My Teacher:_____

Big6

Number One:

What do I need to do?

_____

_____

_____

What questions do I need or want to find out?

1. _____
2. _____
3. _____
4. _____
5. _____
6. _____
7. _____
8. _____

Big 6

Number Two:

What can I use to find what I need?

_____

_____

_____

_____

_____

_____

Number Three:
Where can I find what I need?

- ☐ in the classroom
- ☐ in the library
- ☐ in the lab
- ☐ at home

- ☐ in the library
- ☐ in the classroom
- ☐ at home

- ☐ use the telephone with help of an adult
- ☐ invite to school
- ☐ send an email with help of an adult

 Number Four:
What information can I use?

Write question #1 here:	Write question #2 here:
Answer—	Answer—
Source used: _____	Source used: _____
Write question #3 here:	Write question #4 here:
Answer—	Answer—
Source used: _____	Source used: _____

Write question #5 here:	Write question #6 here:
Answer-	Answer-
Source used: _____	Source used: _____
Write question #7 here:	Write question #8 here:
Answer-	Answer -
Source used: _____	Source used: _____

Big6

Number Five:
How can I show what
I learned?

Write a _____

_____

Use a computer to _____

_____

Show _____

_____

Tell about _____

_____

_____

Make a _____

_____

Big6

Number Five:
These are the sources
I used to find information.

_____

_____

_____

_____

_____

_____

_____

_____

_____

_____

 Number Six:
How will I know if I did well?

1. What did I learn?

2. How well did I do on my _____?

Great! I did my best work! Pretty Well. I almost did my best work. Not very well. I could do better. I did not try hard and did not do my best.

3. Did I include the things I found out about my _____?

Yes! I included everything! I left out one or two facts. I did not include the facts I found.

4. Did I work well with my Big6 Buddy?

Yes!

Most of the
time.

No.

5. What did I do well this time?

6. What could I do better next time?

7. What did I like most about doing this project?

Appendix F
Writing Process Organizer for Grades 2-3

Big6 #1: Task Definition—What do I need to do?

This is the beginning of the first step of the writing process: *Prewriting*

1. What does your teacher want you to do? Ask your teacher to explain if you don't understand.

    Write what it is you are supposed to do (in your own words):

2. What information do you need to include in your writing assignment? Ask your teacher if you don't know. Write a list of questions here so you will know what information to "look up" for your paper:

    1.
    2.
    3.
    4.
    5.
    6.
    7.
    8.

3. Put a check mark by any question above in which you will need to find answers in sources such as books, people, and Web sites.

Big6 #2: Information Seeking Strategies—What can I use to find what I need?

1. You need to make a list of all the possible sources of information (such as books and Web sites) that will help you answer the questions you checked in Big6 #1 *Task Definition* above. Ask your teacher, your librarian, or another adult to help you.

    Make a list here:

2. Now, place a check mark beside each item to which you have access and are able to use. Ask your librarian for help if needed.

Big6 #3: Location and Access—Where can I find what I need?

1. Figure out where you will get these sources. Beside each source in Big6 #2, write its location. If it is a Web site, list its Web address. Try to use those Web sites to which your school subscribes. Ask your librarian about these. This will save you time. If your source is a person, figure out how you will contact him or her and make a note of this.

2. Now, you will actually get the sources. You may have to get and use them one at a time. If so, come back to this step to locate each source.

3. Once you have the source in hand, you must get to the information within the source. Ask your librarian, teacher, or parent for help if needed.

Big6 #4: Use of Information—What information can I use?

1. Read, view, or listen to the sources you have located above.

2. Take notes on paper or a notecard to answer the questions you wrote in Big6 #1. Write only the words that answer your questions.

3. You must give credit to your sources. Ask for help if needed.

Big6 #5: Synthesis—How can I put my information together?

Now it is time to complete the writing process. You should talk to your teacher or librarian if you need help with this.

1. *Prewriting:* You have already completed the note taking part of this step. Now you need to brainstorm (make a list of) original ideas you will include in your paper. Write your ideas on note cards or notebook paper.

2. *Drafting:* Write the first version of your paper. Be sure to include the notes you took from your sources. Make sure you give credit to the books, people, and Web sites you used.

3. *Conferring*: Ask your teacher to talk to you about your paper. Be prepared with at least two questions you would like answered about your paper.

4. *Revising:* During this part of the process, look at and think about what you have written. Your paper should be more than other people's ideas or what you found in Web sites. It should include a lot of your original ideas as well. Make sure it is what your teacher wants you to do for the paper. Make changes to make it better.

   You may want to combine short sentences and begin to look at your use of grammar. Revision makes good writing even better.

   You may need to talk to your teacher again after you revise your paper. Again, have one or two questions ready to ask about your paper.

5. *Editing:* This may be the most important part of the process. Your teacher or other trusted adult should give you ideas about improving your grammar and spelling, if needed. You must correct all errors.

6. *Publishing:* Try to use a word processor to write your final paper. If you don't have a computer, print or write neatly. Make sure you include a list of the

books, people, and Web sites you used. This is called a bibliography. The bibliography should be alphabetized by author. Ask your teacher or librarian if you do not know how to write a bibliography.

Does your teacher also want you to make a product to go with your paper? Now is the time to make it.

**Even though there are several steps to the writing process, it is very important you talk to an adult at each step and understand that you can go back to and repeat any step at any time during the process.

Big6 #6: Evaluation—How will I know if I did well?

Before you show your paper (and product) to others, be sure it is as perfect as you can make it. This paper should be something you are proud to put your name on. Answer "yes" to all of these questions **before** you turn in your paper:

1. Did you do everything and include all that was required for the paper?
2. Does your final paper show your original ideas as well as other information you found?
3. Did you give credit to all of your sources, including a written bibliography?
4. Did you use a word processor to write your paper (or is it very neatly typed or hand-written if you do not have access to a computer)?
5. Is your paper complete and does it include a title page with heading information (title, your name, your teacher's name, date, and other information your teacher wants)?
6. If your teacher asks for these, did you include your notes, copies of each version of your paper, and your list of books, people, and Web sites?
7. Would you be proud for anyone to read this paper?
8. Do you understand each step of the Big6 and writing processes? If not, who can you ask for help?

Works consulted:

Carroll, Joyce Armstrong and Edward E. Wilson. *Acts of Teaching: How to Teach Writing*. Englewood, CO: Teacher Idea Press, 1993.

McGhee, Marla W. Assistant Professor. Educational Administration and Psychological Services, Southwest Texas State University, San Marcos, Texas. Telephone interview. 7 Nov. 2002.

Big6 copyright Eisenberg and Berkowitz, 1987. Organizer copyright Jansen, 2002.

Appendix G
Instructional Unit Planning Guide
for Primary Grades

Unit or curriculum standard:

Information Problem—How can the unit (or specific curriculum standard) be presented as an authentic and/or motivating information problem for students to engage? The problem should cause students to need to and want to engage in the content.

Big6 #1: What do we need to do?

What is the students' task?

How will you introduce it to them? (Check all that apply)

___ Big6 Song

___ Use a puppet

 Which one(s)?

___ Read or tell a story

 Which one?

___ Other—explain:

What information do the students need to know in order to accomplish the task? (List these in question form.) Use the other side if necessary.

Who is responsible for this step? ___teacher ___librarian ___both

Big6 #2: What sources can we use to find what we need?

List sources students will use:

How will students obtain a list of sources?

____ Whole class brainstorming with teacher/librarian guidance

____ Teacher/librarian gives a list of sources

Who will evaluate Web sites for authority and accuracy?

____ teacher

____ librarian

Who is responsible for this step? ___teacher ___librarian ___both

Big6 #3: Where will we find what we need?

How will students locate the sources?

____ Teacher/librarian will locate and show students how sources were located

____ Big6 Buddies will find sources with their Little Buddies

____ Students will locate the sources with the guidance of their teacher/librarian

If students are locating their own sources, what instruction do they need?

Who is responsible for this step? ___teacher ___librarian ___both

Big6 #4: What information can we use?

How will students engage in the source? (Read, listen, view, touch, etc.)

____ teacher/librarian will read as students listen

____ Big6 Buddies will read as students listen

____ students will read with the help of teacher/librarian or other adult

How will students take from the source the information they need (note taking)?

_____ teacher or librarian will take notes on chart paper or other

_____ Big6 Buddies will take notes

_____ students will take notes with the guidance of teacher/librarian or other adult

Which type of organizer will students use to record notes?

_____ data chart

_____ large paper

_____ other

Who is responsible for this step? ___teacher ___librarian ___both

Big6 #5: What will we make to show what we learned?

How will students organize the information from all of their sources?

_____ written rough draft with guidance of teacher/librarian
    or Big6 Buddy

_____ sketch

_____ other

How will students display their results?

_____ product

What is it? (consider having each student write about their results in addition to making an individual or group product)

_____ presentation

    What is it?

_____ other

What higher-level thinking and transferable skills are included in the final product?

What materials and instruction will students need?

Will students choose their own product (with or without guidance)?

How will students give credit to their sources?

_____ simple bibliography

_____ spoken credit during a presentation

Who is responsible for this step? ___teacher ___librarian ___both

Big 6 #6: How will we know if we did well?

How will student evaluate their own efforts?

_____ informal written evaluation

_____ simple checklist provided by teacher or librarian

_____ other

Who is responsible for this step? ___teacher ___librarian ___both

Additional Considerations

What are the content objectives?

What are the specific information problem-solving (Big6) objectives on which you will focus?

What prerequisite skills or content objectives do students need before beginning this sequence of instruction?

What audience will the students have for their efforts?

How will the teacher and librarian be involved with the class or individuals while the other is teaching?

How are the students going to be grouped?

_____ individual

_____ pair

_____ other

What materials are needed and who is responsible for collecting them?

What is the time frame?

How will the unit be evaluated by the teacher and/or librarian?

How will you celebrate and/or advertise the students' products or performances and information searching accomplishments?

Appendix H
Evaluating Units of Instruction

The last project is turned in and the final presentation given. Students have even evaluated their own efforts based on the rubric or scoring guide you provided them. All is said and done. Or is it? How can we ensure that the objectives were met and the best possible instruction presented to the students?

How do teachers and library media specialists new to the Big6 know if the units they design provide the most effective and efficient levels of engagement for their students? How often do those of us who have experience implementing the Big6 actually evaluate our efforts and specifically analyze each step before we present to students? We may informally evaluate our efforts after students complete the unit, but rarely do we do this before teaching. It is with this in mind that I created the Big6 Unit Evaluation Guide. Its purpose is to ensure we leave nothing out of each step so students receive the best possible instruction we can give.

I use the guide to design effective units. It includes the components of higher-level, integrated instruction and transferable skills. Of course, each of the items included won't be appropriate for all units. You will want to modify this guide for individual units and for your teaching style, as well as the needs of individual students and classes. However, use caution when omitting or changing too much—it is easy to end up with a superficial series of activities for students.

The guide begins with two simple questions: Are you using the terminology of the Big6 with students and do they know that they are engaged in a process as they learn the content? I find that teachers will often forget to articulate the correct labels for each step so that in subsequent units students are not aware they are using the same process. You want to articulate the correct terminology so students eventually internalize the steps and understand that the process remains the same when the content changes.

Creating a good problem for Big6 #1 *Task Definition* sets the stage for a successful and engaging unit. There are three main considerations here: First, is the task engaging for students, requiring higher-level thought? Do students have an opportunity to figure out what they need and want to know before you give them a list of information to locate? And, is the task closely tied with the state or school's curriculum standards? Many times we get caught up in designing units of instruction that we love to teach but are not included in the grade's required curriculum.

Carefully evaluating Big6 #2 *Information Seeking Strategies* allows for the use of a variety of accurate and authoritative print and digital resources. Of importance here is the evaluation of sites located on the free Web. Some prefer to include Web evaluation in Big6 #4 *Use of Information*, as one must locate and begin to read the Web site in order to evaluate it for accuracy, authority, and relevance. What matters most is that someone evaluates sites on the free Web, whether it occurs in *Information Seeking Strategies* or *Use of Information*.

Big6 #3 *Location and Access* includes identifying the skills that we should teach in order for students to locate print and digital resources and access information within each. Evaluating Big6 #4 *Use of Information* ensures that we teach efficient note taking skills and developmentally appropriate ways to cite sources.

Three important factors are included in Big6 #5 *Synthesis* to ensure that you design a final product that allows students to add value to the information they found. We want our students to go beyond the facts and other's ideas by showing evidence of higher-level and original thinking. In addition, students should learn transferable skills as they show their results such as technology, composition, production, performance, and presentation skills. Last, students must give credit to their sources.

The final step of the Big6 process, Big6 #6 *Evaluation*, suggests that students write about their experiences in an informal self-evaluation. Additionally, we want to include a set of predetermined criteria, probably the same one that the teacher will use for assessment, such as a rubric, scoring guide, or checklist. This demystifies the expectations for the students and gives them a guideline to follow as they progress through the steps of the process. Typically this is given during *Task Definition* and used as an instrument for self-evaluation.

Using this Big6 Unit Evaluation Guide, or a modification of it, will ensure that your students are engaging in meaningful instruction, resulting in higher-level thinking and efficient and effective information searching and processing.

Evaluating Big6™ Units

Use this guide as you are developing Big6 units for your curriculum standards or objectives. You may find that some of the items below do not meet the needs of particular objectives, however by checking as many as possible, you will ensure that you are designing an effective and engaging unit of instruction.

___ Are you using the Big6 terminology with the students (Task Definition, Information Seeking Strategies, etc.) as you take them through the process?

___ Do your students know that they are using a process to find and use information when they are engaging in Big6 units and that this process can be used any time they need information for a task or problem?

Task Definition—What do we need to do?

1.1 ___ Is the task or information problem engaging?
___ Will students want to study the content?
___ Is the task developmentally appropriate?
___ Does the task require students to think on a higher level?

1.2 ___ Do students have an opportunity to construct what they want to know?
___ Do they think they need to know about the topic before you tell them what they need to find out about it?
___ Is the task written in question format for ease of use?
___ Is the task closely tied to the state or school's curriculum standards?
___ Does it reflect the higher-level thinking of the standards?

Information Seeking Strategies—What can we use to find what we need?

Are the resources:
___ developmentally appropriate?
___ readily available and easy to access?
___ accessible to students who may not read on grade level? Who is able to help them?
___ accurate, authoritative, and relevant?
___ Are students using a variety of resources?
___ Are students using a combination of digital and print resources as appropriate?
___ Which online sources (subscription-based and free Web) will your class use to complete the project?
___ How are students evaluating sites on the free Web, or are you giving them the sites they are to use?
___ Are you evaluating sites on the free Web that the students will use? (this may be performed in Big6 #4: Use of Information)

Location and Access—Where can we find what we need?

3.1 ___ Are you teaching or reviewing how to locate the resources?

3.2 ___ How are students accessing information within the materials? How do you know they will succeed at this?

Use of Information—What information can we use?

4.1 ___ How do you know students will be able to access the section of the resource in which the information appears?

4.2 ___ Are you teaching or reviewing how to take notes? ___ Cite sources? ___ What type of note taking organizer are students using?

Synthesis—How can we show what we learned?

5.1 ___ How are students organizing information from a variety of sources?

5.2 ___ How are students showing evidence of higher-level thinking in the creation of the final product?

___ Are students learning transferable skills (technology, composition, production, performance, presentation) in the creation of their final product?

___ How are students giving credit to the sources they used?

Evaluation—How will we know if we did well?

___ Do students have an informal, written self-evaluation of their efforts?

___ Do students have a set of pre-determined criteria to judge their efforts in a more formal way (such as a rubric, scoring guide, or checklist)? This is the instrument you will use to give them their grade(s). This instrument will usually be given during the Task Definition phase of the assignment.

After unit has been completed:

How successful was this Big6 unit? Will you teach it again?

How successful was the level of student engagement?

How effectively were the learning objectives or standards met?

How successful was your collaboration with the school library media specialist or classroom teacher(s) in the completion of this project?

What do you need to consider or change the next time you teach this unit?

Index

Dewey Decimal Classification system, teaching, 35, 163
differentiating instruction, 37, 39, 43, 45, 120
    definition, 43
Discoverer, 68
Do We Really Know Dewey, 164
domains, learning, 26

E

early learners
    accomplishments of, 26
    use of technology, 32
EBSCO, 132
EBSCOhost, 60, 68, 92
Education Digest, 48
Educational Leadership, 48
Eisenberg, Laura, 23
Eisenberg, Michael B., xiv, 23
eLibrary Elementary, 60, 68
encyclopedia skills
    choosing between a book and an
        encyclopedia, 61
    choosing the correct volume, 70
    locating an article, 69
    locating articles, 69
engaging information, 18, 52
essential points of access, 17, 71, 72, 80
    for new readers, 71
    for non- and emerging readers, 71
Evaluation, xi, xiii, 5, 6, 12, 21, 22, 36, 42, 63, 94, 95, 96, 102, 123, 128, 129, 134, 138, 146, 147, 149, 152, 158, 161, 182, 185, 187, 188, 190
    checklists, 22, 98
    definition, 21
    examples, 96, 99, 187
    instruction, 95
    planning, 94
    rubrics, 22
    scoring guides, 22

F

Folkmanis puppets, 114
Furgerson, Paige, 47

G

Galdone, Paul, 160
Gale, 68
The Gingerbread Man, 160
Google, 62, 68, 79, 146, 147
Great Web Sites for Kids, 68
groups, determining size, 102
guest speakers, 60, 79

H

higher order thinking. *See* thinking, higher
    order
A Home for Toad, 52, 153, 155

I

If You Were There in 1492, 132
information
    application, 18
    definition, 54

engaging, 18
finding, 126
identifying needed information, 55
identifying the need for, 13
organizing, 190
presenting results, 20
teaching concept to young learners, 54
Information and Communications Technology
    (ICT). *See* technology
information problems. *See* problems,
    information
Information Seeking Strategies, xi, xiii, 5, 6, 11, 12, 15, 34, 62, 137, 146, 147, 161, 180, 187, 187
    engaging non- and emerging readers, 60
    examples, 15
instruction, xii, xiii, 5, 23, 27, 40, 46, 47, 54, 55, 56, 60, 66, 74, 88, 95, 101, 102
    planning, xii, xiii, 26, 50, 120, 183
    planning for differentiated instruction, xii, 43, 44, 45
    process of exclusion, 62, 63, 137
Information Stations, 66, 103, 132, 133, 137
    use of computers, 67, 132
    use of encyclopedias, 69, 132
instruction
    differentiating, 33, 37, 39, 43, 44, 48
interactive writing, xii, 46, 47, 120. *See* also
    Sharing the Pen
    examples, 46

J

Jansen, Barbara A., viii, 23, 47, 58, 63, 72, 85, 96, 97, 98, 99, 118, 119, 129, 153
Johnson, Margaret J., 47

K

keywords, 35, 71, 80
Kid's InfoBits, 68
KidPix, 21, 36, 44, 45, 88, 89, 126, 128
KidsClick, 17, 68, 132, 146
Kidspiration, 45, 57, 58, 84
King, Coretta Scott, Awards, 150
Kostelnik, Marjorie J., 37
KWL, 54, 55, 145

L

Lander, Brenda, 103, 104
Lauer, Diane, 63
The Learning Company, 126
learning domains
    Big6 focus on, 26, 37
lesson plan ideas
    comparing objects and events of today and
        long ago, 53
    contributions of ordinary people in the
        community, 54
    holidays, 53, 142
    map skills, 53, 116
    natural resources, 54, 71, 91, 124, 125, 126, 136, 137, 138
    pets, 53, 145
    prehistoric animals, 53